CREATE YOUR OWN
STAGE SETS

CREATE YOUR OWN
STAGE SETS
Terry Thomas

A SPECTRUM BOOK

Prentice-Hall, Inc., Englewood Cliffs, New Jersey 07632

Library of Congress Cataloging in Publication Data

Thomas, Terry.
　　Create your own stage sets.

　　(Theatrical staging series)
　　''A Spectrum Book''
　　Includes index.
　　1.　Theaters — Stage-setting and scenery.
　　2.　Amateur theater.　I.　Title.　II.　Series.
PN2091.S8T56　1984　　　792'.025　　　83-21181
ISBN 0-13-189085-9
ISBN 0-13-189077-8 (pbk.)

This book is available at a special discount when ordered in bulk quantities.
Contact Prentice-Hall, Inc., General Publishing Division,
Special Sales, Englewood Cliffs, N.J. 07632.

First published in the USA 1985
Prentice-Hall, Inc.

10 9 8 7 6 5 4 3 2 1

ISBN 0-13-189085-9

ISBN 0-13-189077-8 {PBK.}

Prentice-Hall International, Inc., *London*
Prentice-Hall of Australia Pty. Limited, *Sydney*
Prentice-Hall Canada Inc., *Toronto*
Prentice-Hall of India Private Limited, *New Delhi*
Prentice-Hall of Japan, Inc., *Tokyo*
Prentice-Hall of Southeast Asia Pte. Ltd., *Singapore*
Whitehall Books Limited, *Wellington, New Zealand*
Editora Prentice-Hall do Brasil Ltda., *Rio de Janeiro*

Typesetting by
Avonset, Midsomer Norton, Bath

Printed in Great Britain by
Purnell & Sons (Book Production)
Limited, Paulton.

Create Your Own Stage Sets
was conceived, edited,
and designed by Thames Head Limited,
Avening, Tetbury,
Gloucestershire,
Great Britain

Editor
Alison Goldingham

Consultant editor
Anthony Rowe
Head of Design, Bristol Old Vic Theatre School

Art Editor
Tony De Saulles

Designers and illustrators
Heather Church
Craig Warwick
Bill Padden
Phil Daniels
Jacquie Govier
Nicholas Rous
Terry Thomas
Nick Allen

Contents

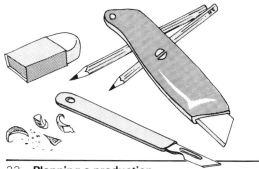

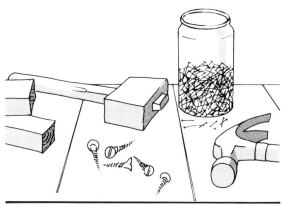

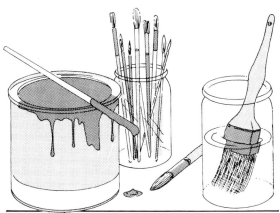

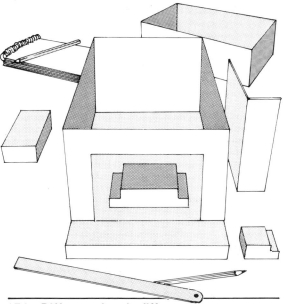

Introduction

The house lights grow dim, conversation slowly subsides, an air of expectation and excitement fills the now darkened auditorium. The curtain rises. An appreciative murmur greets the scenery. Even before a word has been spoken, the set designer has taken his curtain call. The scenery must then become merely a canvas upon which the action of the play is painted.

That brief but savored moment, however, is ample reward for the weeks of effort, the research, design and construction put in by the backstage team. A 'team' it must be. Each member contributing skill and commitment to help interpret the designer's plan. The audience may be unaware of the very real influence of the setting but their enjoyment of the production will be colored by its effectiveness.

The audience will not see the bent nails and pieces of string, the flimsy battlements and less than regal tapestries, but they will enjoy the satisfying environment within which the play is performed. It is the responsibility of the set designer to make sure not only that the set looks right but also that it works well for the director, the cast, the stage crew, as well as the audience.

While the initial design concept is often intuitive, a store of knowledge and practical experience allied to a sense of adventure, will determine how much of that original vision eventually takes shape on the stage.

Whether your playhouse is purpose built, a recreation hall, or simply an open space, you will need basic units, and these must be carefully positioned if the designer is to retain his most valued asset — space.

Every production presents new problems. Too much space is one which rarely besets the amateur. It is more likely that the designer must accommodate a grandiose production on a constrictingly small stage. Use of space will directly affect the actor and the action and every device must be employed to save, create and fully utilize every square inch of the acting area.

Uncluttered space on stage helps the director to maneuver and manipulate the movements of the cast — blocking and grouping in and around a set to give dramatic emphasis.

Scenery also requires a degree of choreography. Here the key man is the stage manager. He manages people, things, and events backstage. He is responsible for the movement of scenery on and off stage so that the pace of the production is maintained. Sadly, some amateur plays are ruined by a loss of tension when undue time is taken to change the sets.

Many well-tried and tested methods of reducing this delay are illustrated in this book. Properly used these devices will create more valuable space on and off stage. The versatility of trucks and wagons also gives continuity and smooth scene changing.

Groups who perform on small stages need not despair. Even the most ambitious production can be mounted with the help of carefully planned models, some ingenuity in construction and good teamwork backstage. Sometimes the humble caster and hinge answer all the needs of the set builder who lacks operating space.

The construction of stage scenery can be particularly satisfying and the stage team should aim to build well, economically and accurately. Unlike the professional theater, the amateur stage cannot afford to make many special 'one-off' units. The stock furniture of the stage (flats, rostra, curtains and cloths) must be used and re-used many times and needs to be well made and robust. Time is much better spent making carefully constructed units than by carrying out last minute repairs to more flimsy pieces. Exploit stock units to the full before embarking on ambitious new constructions.

Nevertheless, there are occasions when a specially designed piece of scenery is necessary as the centerpiece of a design. This gives the stage carpenter considerable pleasure and adds an extra dimension to the building program. The much increased availability of power tools has eased the work of the set builders. The speed of construction enables the director and cast to become acquainted with the shape of the set at a much earlier point. Investment in Club tools is worthwhile expenditure. Although most practical members have their own tool sets, the availability of equipment in the workshop eliminates delay.

Safety

Accidents can all too easily occur. Make safety a priority, wear sensible clothes and provide sturdy and level work surfaces. Always switch off the electricity after using power tools, and remove the plug. Ventilate the working area to disperse fumes. Keep a first aid box properly filled. Replace tools after use in adequate shelving or in cupboards. The department head is responsible for maintaining the tools and it is worth remembering that blunt tools are as dangerous as sharp ones.

Fireproofing

All stage settings must be fireproofed. Fireproofing crystals can be bought ready for use or a solution can be made up from 15 ounces (425g) of boracic-acid crystals and 10 ounces (283g) of sodium phosphate in a gallon (4 ls) of water. Be careful how you spray the solution, for colors may run or delicate shapes may be damaged.

◇ Look out for the hazard symbols throughout the book, which identify potentially dangerous situations.

Licences and permissions

Write to the publishers for details of licence and fees.

The language of the Stage

The terminology used in the theater has developed over many years. Some phrases have entered the language, 'to upstage', 'in the limelight', 'on cue', are understood by all, but much of the vocabulary remains the preserve of those intimately involved in the theater.

This jargon can dissuade enthusuastic newcomers and even confuse less experienced members. In the following pages those expressions will be used freely, but it will make easier reading if you first consult the glossary on page 188.

As all backstage work demands swift, efficient and silent teamwork, common description and understanding among the crew will contribute to a smooth running production.

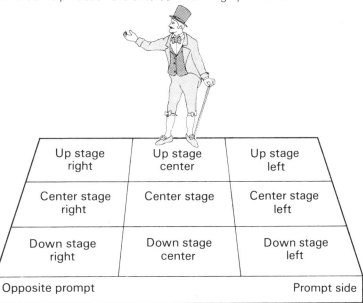

Up stage right	Up stage center	Up stage left
Center stage right	Center stage	Center stage left
Down stage right	Down stage center	Down stage left

| Opposite prompt | | Prompt side |

The theater past and present

To most people the theater means the type of playhouse so firmly established in the nineteenth century. However, the word 'theater' is derived from the Greek *theatrum* meaning 'a viewing place' and it is this Victorian interpretation of 'viewing' which has so conditioned our ideas on the presentation of drama.

Theater architects of that time designed the proscenium arch and auditorium in a heavily decorated style. Red velvet seats and curtains, gilded neo-classical statues and sparkling chandeliers featured prominently, to create an illusion of luxury. The proscenium arch became transformed into a picture frame in which were depicted scenes as near reality as possible. The artificiality was disguised, the workmanship and mechanics of staging hidden, and the audience kept at arm's length beyond the footlights.

Recent years have seen many changes in theater design and building. Now that audiences can see 'the real thing' on a television or cinema screen, they expect more stimulation and less visual deception from the theater. The professional theater has been forced to develop quite different methods of presentation where the involvement of the audience is a more integral part. These changes, far from being adventurous or avant-garde, reveal a need to rediscover the true mystery of drama.

The relaxing of convention has been of great benefit to the amateur, who is beginning to experiment with a broader approach. Arena, theater in the round, thrust stages, and rough theater are all presentation techniques which can be added to the tried and tested conventional proscenium arch.

The designer's task is to present the cast's best efforts in the most effective way. Whatever the dimensions of the building, and within economic and structural bounds, be prepared to experiment. The audience's ability to see and hear is far more important than scenery or the actors' convenience.

Theater in the round

Arena amphitheater

The states of Greece and Rome recognized and accommodated the fusion that joins performer to audience. Their theaters were centers of spectacle and ritual. Contests of skill, religious ritual, gladiatorial combat, as well as drama took place in these multipurpose arenas.

The Greeks fashioned their theaters from the natural contours of the land. They built into hillsides and the shape produced remarkable acoustical qualities. A person standing at the foot of the hill, even when speaking in a whisper, can be heard by everyone in the audience.

Although the Romans, who were skilled engineers and builders, constructed vast concrete arenas to house spectacular events, the principle remained the same, everyone could see and be seen, could hear and be heard!

Today that principle of maximum visibility is relatively simple to apply. Surround the acting arena with seating — raised on rostra if possible. Allow space for entrances. Set the lighting high and direct it on to the acting area. Avoid positioning peripheral light that can shine into the faces of the audience. The need for scenery is

Greek theater

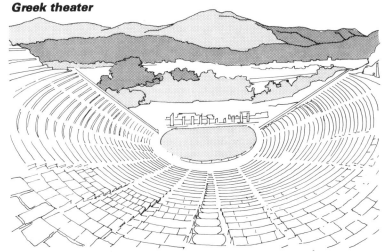

Spectators looked down upon a circle of raised earth called the 'orchestra'. The actors changed costume in a temporary wooden structure set behind, known as the 'skena'

minimal — low, simple units will suffice. This enables costume, color and movement to influence the course of the play.

This type of production eliminates many of the problems that beset designers faced with more traditional stages.

If you have tiered, or raked, seating, little apart from simple properties is required. The audience is, for the most part, looking down on the action. However, some form of platform

does give the players a sense of position, particularly if there are several points of access to the acting area.

The absence of tiered seating causes a loss of vision for the audience. In this case a low platform — 24 to 30 inches (60 — 70 cm) high is recommended. The dimensions of this platform will depend upon the space available, of course, and the allowance of 3 to 4 feet (90 — 120 cm) as a floor level apron.

Check the sight-lines to ensure that the action is seen from every seat in the arena

Construction of the platform

Slotted lengths of angled steel or a scaffolding structure are ideal for the platform. They may be constructed and taken down without the consequent storage problem created by fixed rostra. The acting surface should be secured by wooden-retaining blocks on the underside and made wider than the subframe so that a skirt can be attached easily. Before beginning the construction ensure that protective plywood 'pads' cover the auditorium floor beneath each vertical post.

It is advisable to lay a stage cloth or carpet on the platform to reduce noise levels. Use existing stock rostra to create a variety of levels, and steps and ramps for access. Ramps take up more space but facilitate movement on and off the stage.

Always remember that the audience must see all the action. Scene changes can be easily and unobtrusively made by minor rearrangement of the items and means of access on the platform.

The central platform provides a variety of acting levels. The interest is centered on the actors with no distracting scenery

A modern reconstruction of the successful Greek formula. Use the many entrances and exits to full advantage in your production

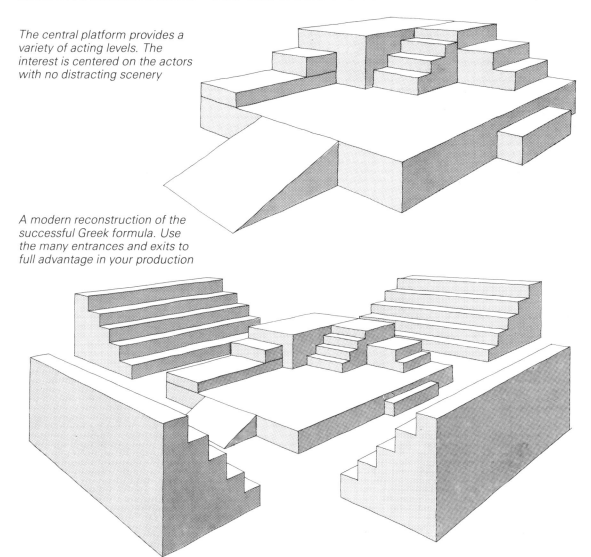

Thrust stage theater

In Elizabethan England, actors were homeless. Groups of traveling players performed where they could — on village greens, at fairs, in guild-halls or inn yards. They acted out interludes or plays between the courses of banquets in great houses. Judged 'rogues and vagabonds or sturdie beggars' unless they could prove that they were in the paid service of a nobleman, they carried their stage or scaffold from place to place. This scaffold was a simple arrangement of basic poles and planking easily erected and just as swiftly dismantled.

This method of presentation has been revived and become a very effective arrangement. It has numerous advantages, not the least of which is the increased proximity of the audience to the performer. The wide range of possible entrances involves the audience still further. Scenery may still be set on the stage but it becomes less important than costume, properties and lighting in creating visual interest and atmosphere. The stage floor, too, becomes more prominent. Ideally seating should be raked, as this improves vision all around.

There are some drawbacks to be considered with this stage arrangement: It restricts the number of seats. Local fire regulations may insist on extra gangway spacing. Contrasting scene changes are awkward. Front curtains are no longer front! Set rearrangement can be achieved by the stage team but they may need to be dressed in costume. Sight-lines, both vertical and horizontal, are greatly extended. Nevertheless the advantages often outweigh these administrative factors.

Look at your playhouse. Calculate the cost in lost revenue, and balance the novelty and challenge of the thrust stage arrangement against a traditional proscenium arched presentation.

A versatile and easily erected scaffold used by traveling players

The Globe

The Globe theater in London, was designed in wood and built on the South Bank of the Thames among cockfighting arenas and bear baiting pits. The circular layout of the auditorium was retained and the traditional scaffold, much enlarged, was set within the circle. The audience was arranged in galleries around this thrusting rectangle

With seats on three sides the thrust stage can assume a great variety of forms. Entrances can be made from the audience tunnels, sides, through the stage floor and from the back

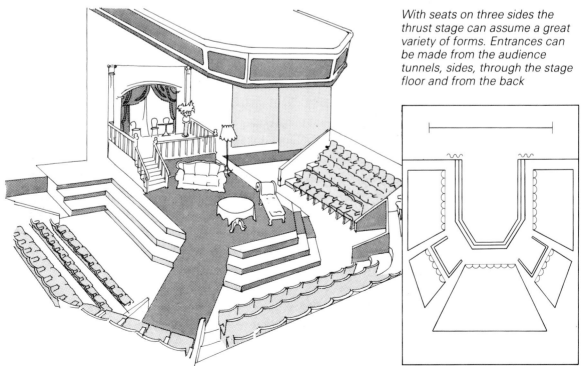

Proscenium theater

The accession to the English Throne of James I effectively ended the particularly Elizabethan style of theatrical presentation.

Inigo Jones, a brilliant engineer and famous impresario was commissioned to design and present lavish masques with elaborate and fantastic settings for the pleasure of the King and his court. Whilst Shakespeare had used language and imagination to paint the scene, Inigo Jones used back-cloths, flats and the illusion of perspective on his *machina versatilis* to bewitch the audience. All this was framed within an ornamental arch which closely resembled the triumphal arches of the Roman emperors and Renaissance princes. It was called the proscenium arch (latinized from the Greek *proskenion,* in front of the stage) and became the dominant design of theater for years to follow.

As theater design became more formalized around this construction and scenery became ever more a mirror on nature, the proscenium arch distanced the action from the audience. They observed the play from the 'fourth wall' of the setting depicted on the stage. The auditorium rose from the stalls to circle and gallery and the stage floor was tilted or raked towards it. The expressions 'up stage' and 'down stage' were born as a result of this angled floor construction. Plays were written with this stage structure in mind and although the box setting has become tired through over-use the concepts still work.

Wing space seems always to be at a premium and as access to both sides of the stage is necessary for both actor and stage team during the action, take care to avoid cluttering this area with scenery or props. The visual 'punctuation' in the proscenium is provided by the front traverse tabs (curtains). These need to be smooth running. A heavy cloth is recommended for both front traverse tabs and wing or leg curtains. Extra weight can be added by putting lead shot into the bottom hems. (The various track and bracket systems are dealt with on page 92.) Other traverse tabs or rolled back-cloths can be positioned along the stage ceiling to facilitate scene changes and to vary the acting area.

Do not feel obliged to stay within the arch. Go beyond it, add to it, change its shape. Be prepared to

An elaborate Victorian proscenium arch setting

experiment. It will prove to be an experience for both audience and actors alike.

Today the disciplines stemming from the proscenium style need no longer prevail. At its most basic, a proscenium arched stage needs only a back wall and simple side curtaining to provide a neutral background for the acting area.

The cyclorama or sky-cloth allows the designer to give an illusion of great distance on stage. A stage apron extended into the auditorium breaks the picture frame effect by bringing the action into the auditorium. Entrances and exits made through the audience help carry the audience into and out of the artificial enclosure made by the arch.

If you can govern the design of the proscenium arch, make it as high as possible. It enlarges the design capability and adds the extra dimension of different acting levels. Vertical sight-lines are extended and encourage the eye to move away from a flat stage arrangement.

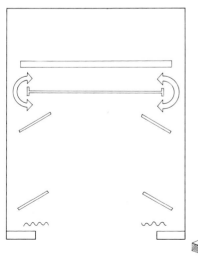

The basic frame through which all the action is viewed does not have to be restricting

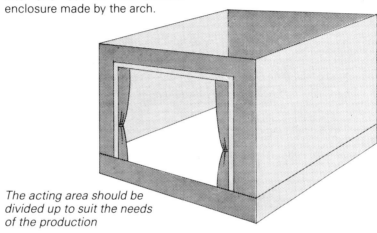

The acting area should be divided up to suit the needs of the production

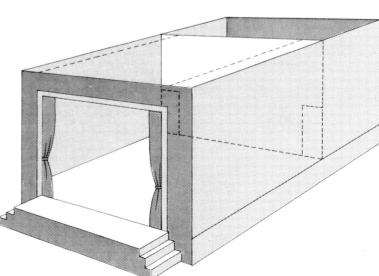

Backstage space, wing space and ceiling space will influence the flexibility of the set design

Theater in the open air

One of the most beautiful of outdoor theaters lies near Land's End in Cornwall, England: the Mynack Theatre at Porthcurno which faces the sea. Here the natural shape of the cliff has been transformed into a theater, by cutting tiers of seating into the rock. The 'stage' is a grassy level furnished simply with a low balustrade and a variety of stone blocks which serve as tables and seats. It is a thrilling experience to watch a performance set against a backdrop of sea, cliffs and sky. Here, as in many other outdoor settings, Nature has designed the perfect set.

Gardens, yards, housefronts and courtyards all make good settings as long as certain points are kept in mind.

Make good use of what you have in a garden: bushes, hedges and trees can be real allies. Avoid a sometimes unhappy marriage between real and imitation. If you need to create additional effects with stage flats, or a profile requires alteration, make absolutely sure that these additions are anchored securely on a scaffold base. Even the lightest gust of wind can play havoc with flimsy stage material.

The architecture of a house may be ideal for your setting, if properly lit. A housefront can make an impressive backdrop with natural entrances, but beware of western windows. At sunset, reflections can be very distracting for the audience.

Try to avoid gravel or surfaces with loose chippings. The conflict between footsteps and speech can cause problems.

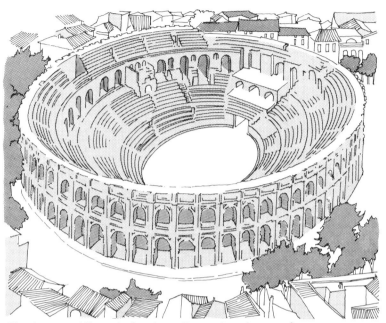

The Arena at Nîmes in Southern France is only one of many magnificent open air theaters built by the Romans. Many thousands of spectators could witness gladiatorial combat and contest. Today, bullfights and ice shows are presented throughout the summer

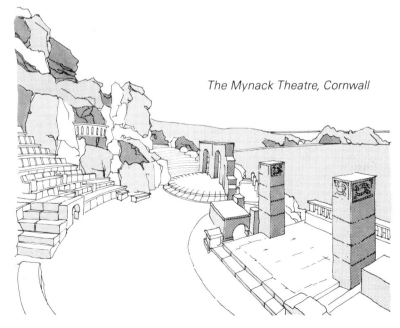

The Mynack Theatre, Cornwall

Hidcote Gardens, Gloucestershire — perhaps one of the finest outdoor theaters, set in the grounds of a country manor

Lighting

Light sources should be positioned subtly — behind bushes or hedges, in trees and behind walls. Simple screens may be used sparingly to complement natural barriers.

Evening performances need stage lighting: Stage lighting requires power cables. Arrange them safely and unobtrusively. If a generator is used, make sure it is well away from the acting area and, if possible, fence it in. This will help 'baffle' the sound of the running motor.

After the performance, don't forget to make good any damage caused and to thank your hosts — you may wish to repeat the exercise!

Acting area

Lighting

Seating

Concourse

Your theater

It is indeed a fortunate theater group that has a permanent home. Too often the group must share a building with other groups whose interests differ greatly. Public rooms often present an unhappy compromise. Planning and forethought can find solutions to the problems posed, however, and those very problems help generate an originality of presentation. Certain essential questions need to be answered. Make sure all departments of the theater group are aware of and are prepared to deal with design obstacles before making any preliminary sketches or plans.

Let's begin by supposing that your group has just been formed. Enthusiasm runs high. The following are some key areas for investigation and discussion, school halls, village halls, gymnasiums, community centers, Alternative Theater spaces, are all intended to accommodate many forms of group activity. The awareness of fire hazards in public buildings has justified certain safety regulations — the width of walkways, the provision of fire fighting equipment, the number and positioning of fire exits are stipulated by law. Arrange a meeting with the local fire prevention officer to discuss these regulations.

The availablity of community halls is critical. How soon prior to a performance can you begin setting the stage? What other activities precede and follow the production? What are the rental charges? Is there sufficient suitable seating?

There may well be an important basketball game or an antique fair beforehand, public meetings during, and a disco immediately after, your proposed dates! Make contingency plans for these events well in advance.

Accessibility

If scenic units, flats, rostra and so on are to be built away from the venue, carefully measure the height and width of entrances, the length and angles of corridors and the size of the acting area so that the units may be constructed with confidence.

Structural aspects

If you intend to use the hall on a regular basis, negotiate fixed terms and operating practices with the authority concerned. Will you be allowed to alter the stage, fit permanent machinery within the stage area, and add more doors if necessary? Check also that the roof is load bearing.

Power

Stage lighting makes great demands on the power supply and wiring. Should more power points be needed, can you obtain an effective, economic on and off stage power supply?

The stage

Although most multipurpose halls have a skeleton stage, it may need enlarging or extending. Will existing rostra be strong enough to bear extra weight and activity? Can they be effectively secured?

How wide, how high and how deep is the stage? If it has an existing proscenium arch, has it an efficient curtain track, will you need to erect extra traverse curtain rail?

All these factors will influence your mode of presentation. A low ceiling will determine the extent to which you may 'fly' scenery and narrow wing space will hinder all but the simplest of set changes.

Off stage

The building of thrust or extended stage aprons intrudes into the auditorium and restricts and governs the seating capacity. This in turn dictates the size of audience and of course its related ticket income.

When everyone in the group is familiar with the possibilities of your 'theater', then suitable productions can be planned with more background knowledge.

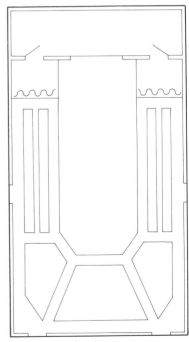

Plan view of a thrust stage arrangement which is easily incorporated into a community hall. The audience has excellent vision, but seating capacity is restricted

A multipurpose hall

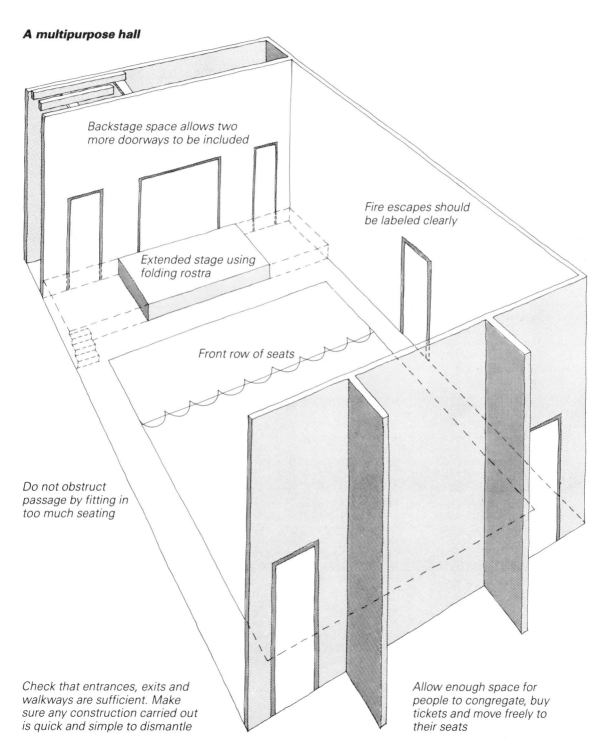

Backstage space allows two more doorways to be included

Fire escapes should be labeled clearly

Extended stage using folding rostra

Front row of seats

Do not obstruct passage by fitting in too much seating

Check that entrances, exits and walkways are sufficient. Make sure any construction carried out is quick and simple to dismantle

Allow enough space for people to congregate, buy tickets and move freely to their seats

Planning a production

In the perfect drama group, the level of enthusiasm and commitment is maintained at a high level with frequent successful and fulfilling productions building up morale throughout the season. Militating against this momentum one must accept the reality of illness, disagreements, frustration and home and work demands, and these problems are best absorbed by a solid management committee.

A separate selection committee of leading members must decide on a well-balanced program with the help of a panel of play readers.

A play is chosen by joint decision and performance dates fixed. A director is appointed who will then recruit a cast and backstage team.

The next step is to arrange meetings with each head of department to discuss interpretation, setting, lighting, costume and color themes, and to identify work priorities.

A timetable should be prepared with regular progress meetings to coordinate each department and to ensure that the work will be completed before the technical rehearsals are due.

The heads of department can then decide on and delegate their creative tasks and produce designs, plans and color schemes for discussion and approval.

The first technical rehearsal follows the 'costume call' and enables the backstage team to run through the lighting and property changes without the cast being present.

At the final technical rehearsal the director checks and confirms lighting levels and times set changes and movement of props.

The dress rehearsal is a performance with no interruptions and is the last opportunity for the director and stage team to iron out operating difficulties and make adjustments before the audience is invited to Opening Night!

Researching the play

Plays are available from leading publishers, libraries, county drama organizations and regular stage magazines. The selection of plays may well be influenced by factors outside the society, for example drama festivals, pantomime and tourist seasons. All plays should be considered on merit, on the ability of the society to stage and cast them satisfactorily, as well as the preferences of the group and the potential audience.

Once you have a play, a director, a cast, a backstage team and a date, you are ready to go. The director will have his own vision and interpretation of the play, which may require a novel treatment — *As You Like It* as he wants it! The designer as well as reflecting this approach must heighten the dramatic quality of the play for the benefit of the audience. If you are the designer, how do you begin?

Read the play, not once but several times. Only by doing so will you understand fully the relationship of word to action and the key elements of sound and vision.

Identify and isolate the period of the play. Collect together as much reference material as you can. Photographs, books, articles, costume, architectural detail, all consolidate the mental picture conjured up by the written word. Register the color — both tonal and emotional — long gowns sweeping over marble floors, mean, dark streets as the backdrop to an angry meeting. Fix in your mind the style, texture and shape of the period, whether it be art nouveau or Gothic splendor, and make frequent rough pencil or water-color sketches of different images and facets of the play.

Take the opportunity to visit appropriate places and buildings. Use your camera!

Immerse yourself in the atmosphere and historical period of the play. Collect as much reference material as possible and make detailed notes

Take into consideration the physical movement of the players. A lady in a bustle walks with greater difficulty than her present day be-jeaned counterpart. Not only must the cast move naturally and with ease, but the scenery too needs careful choreography. Every play has points of climax and key lines. The design task is to build into the setting a variety of levels, entrances and exits which will compliment the text. A 'sad last look back' is more effective if made from an up stage high level facing the audience than at floor level facing into the set.

The fleeing villain should not need the agility of a gymnast to negotiate his escape off stage. The frantic exits and entrances of farce demand doors with ample space on both sides of the set, and a riotous mob lose heart if they have to queue up to leave the stage through a narrow gap.

Stores design their displays with the aid of 'customer flow' charts which help identify the most visited produce sections. In a similar way, a designer must identify from the script, the stage areas in which the most significant parts of the action take place and build his setting to make it easily accessible and dramatically significant. Sketch out a variety of entrances suggested by the plot and experiment with levels to highlight these changes.

The magic of the theater depends on the tension created between actor and audience. The audience will believe what they are told they are seeing if this is expressed with conviction by the actor and style by the designer.

Theater more than any other art form is an overstatement of life!

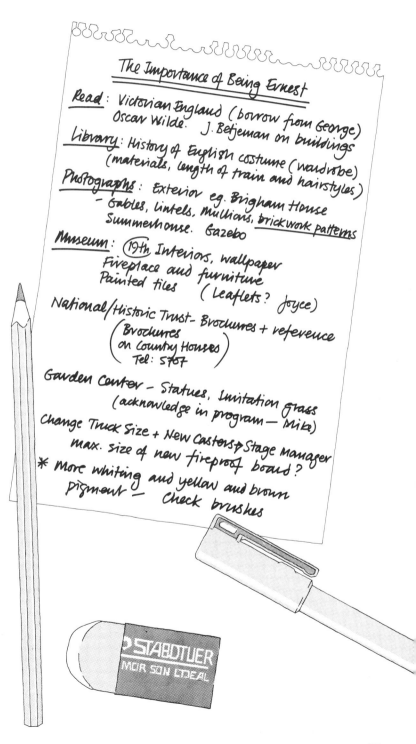

The Importance of Being Ernest

Read: Victorian England (borrow from George)
Oscar Wilde. J. Betjeman on buildings

Library: History of English costume (wardrobe)
(materials, length of train and hairstyles)

Photographs: Exterior eg. Brigham House
- Gables, lintels, mullions, brickwork patterns
Summerhouse. Gazebo

Museum: 19th Interiors, wallpaper
Fireplace and furniture
Painted tiles
(Leaflets? Joyce)

National/Historic Trust- Brochures + reference
(Brochures
on Country Houses)
Tel: 5707

Garden Center - Statues, Imitation grass
(acknowledge in program — Mike)

Change Truck Size + New Casters➔ Stage Manager
max. size of new fireproof board?

* More whiting and yellow and brown
pigment — Check brushes

STAEDTLER
MARS SON IDEAL

The set designer's role

In small drama societies, the luxury of a set designer cannot be afforded. He must double as scene painter, set builder and frequently the assistant stage manager. However this experience helps the designer to maintain a practical approach.

Set design must always be thought of in three dimensions, irrespective of the type of theater. The design must allow movement and action without causing interference or awkwardness.

It cannot be said too often how essential it is that you fully understand the play and read the written text and stage directions carefully. It is helpful to incorporate your own general rough notes and sketches with factual details such as the number of cast, entrances and exits, acting levels and the need for space.

Discuss with the director his interpretation of the play and identify those parts which, because of the limitation of your stage and backstage area, will need re-planning. Often your joint solution to such problems will create a fresh view of the piece.

The next stage is to produce more detailed stage plans and make sketches with a color wash (water-color, gouache, crayon)to show how stage lighting will affect the scenery. When you have established the rough design — research the details of building and decor.

Using stiff paper or cardboard make a simple scale model of the stage. Draw and color in the scenery separately. When dry the cardboard can be shaped to your requirements and set within the stage model (see page 46). (It is probably better not to glue the cardboard to the baseboard until you have discussed the set's workability with the stage manager.)

If it is necessary to build a particular unit the designer will need to draw a detailed sketch showing dimensions. Here again a cardboard model is a valuable aid.

At this point the experienced stage manager can apply his technical knowledge to your theory, a reasonable cost can be estimated for the budget meeting and a working timetable laid down.

The designer must now establish the color and tone values and communicate them to the stage painters, and the costume and props departments. Paint or material samples will help achieve accurate matching.

The designer should continue to produce detailed drawings and models to assist both the stage manager and the director who will be well into cast rehearsal.

Ideally the cast should rehearse on the actual stage to familiarize themselves with the acting area, but this should be avoided while the set is under construction. Rehearsals held on a partly-built setting are fraught with anxiety and in somes cases real danger. The well made model theater is a useful director's aid and colored sketches help the cast to visualize the play as they rehearse.

When the set has been built, rehearse the physical changes of flats (see page 54) and main scenery items with the stage team until the best methods and storage positions have been established. The designer and stage manager can then inspect the set to make small changes — masking gaps, strengthening or toning down the painting, altering angles, to take advantage of the increased stage lighting.

Now the cast can rehearse on the completed set.

Technical rehearsals

Carefully time the act of changing the set and agree the number of hands with the stage manager.

Mark the position of the setting lines on stage with colored adhesive tape (see page 44). Do not overdo this if the stage is bare and the auditorium has steeply raked seating. Small crosses will suffice. Practice the set changes and allocate particular tasks to the assistant stage managers. Do not forget to liase with properties and lighting to avoid collisions.

The final technical rehearsal enables the backstage team to integrate with the cast. The director is able to make final adjustments to ensure that scene changes and climaxes are timed correctly, and that the whole production is co-ordinated.

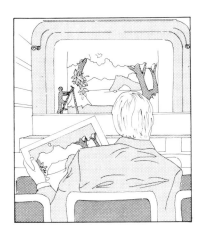

The set designer's role

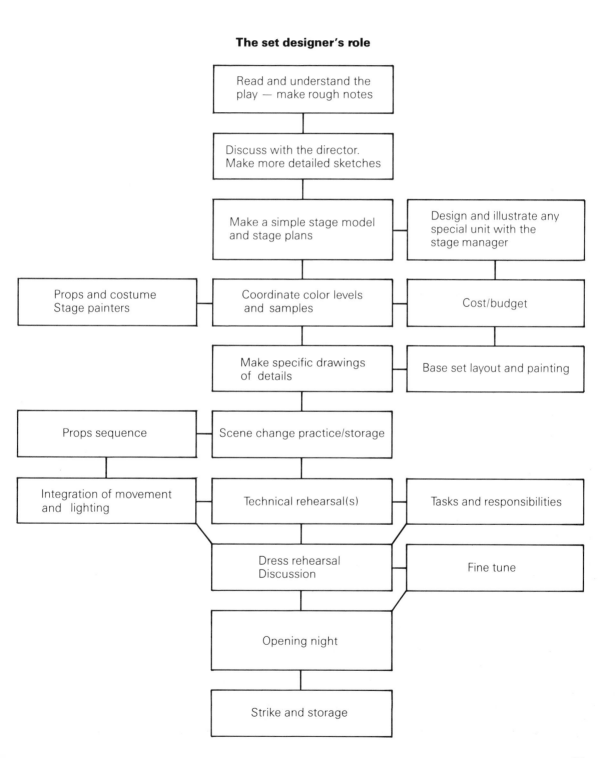

Read and understand the play — make rough notes

Discuss with the director. Make more detailed sketches

Make a simple stage model and stage plans

Design and illustrate any special unit with the stage manager

Props and costume Stage painters

Coordinate color levels and samples

Cost/budget

Make specific drawings of details

Base set layout and painting

Props sequence

Scene change practice/storage

Integration of movement and lighting

Technical rehearsal(s)

Tasks and responsibilities

Dress rehearsal Discussion

Fine tune

Opening night

Strike and storage

General principles of design

The finished work of the designer is, for the audience, the introduction to the play. This first impression sets the mood before the first word is spoken. The designer's influence is felt by the interplay of line, form and color.

Line

The audience is more influenced by the set design than they realise. A strong scenery line will lead the eye into and around the acting area. By its linear and spatial dimensions, the set alone will create mood and atmosphere. Smooth sweeping curves can be calming, whereas sharp angular shapes create tension. Movement from one area to another, accompanied by sympathetic lighting provide a director with the variety and contrast he needs.

Movement

This is a reference not to physical movement but to the pattern of optical signals. The eye movement can be interrupted, countered, or even reversed, by deliberate positioning of scenery or props.

Dimension

The size of one form against another, and the space around and between those forms must relate to the actor. It is the actor who gives a setting its true scale. If the play is based in a castle, the designer must suggest the formidable atmosphere of the building, with the claustrophobic heaviness of cellars or tunnels, or rooftops that give a feeling of height and air. Although form and mass are influenced by color and light, they must first be established.

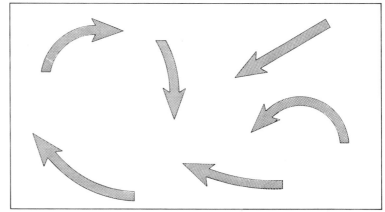

The major lines direct the eye into and around the setting

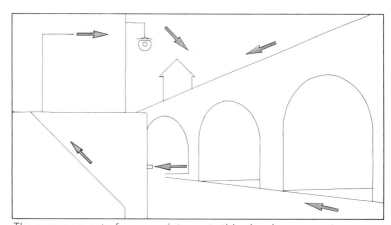

The arrangement of scenery interrupts this visual movement

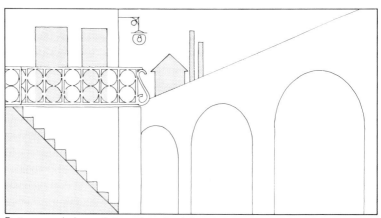

Pattern and shape interact and relate

Color

We will only touch briefly on the contribution of color at the design stage. It is dealt with in greater detail on page 106.

Color on stage can be a powerful stimulus to mood and atmosphere. Study the spectrum. Familiarize yourself with complimentary and contrasting colors and relate them to emotional response: yellow — radiant and light; red — active, warm and dangerous; orange — earthy, cheerful; and blue — cool, pure but passive. Aim for a unity of color but don't overdo it. A visual collision may well suit the mood of the play. At this stage in the design confer with wardrobe and property managers and produce color-washed sketches with more detail. If the water-color technique is not your forte, use water-color crayons. These can be 'washed out' with a paint brush and create good 'lighting' effects.

Light

Light and its versatility of strength and delicacy, its direction and distribution, contributes more than anything to a mood setting.

After making your initial broad sketches, use a bold water-color technique to wash in the lighting effect on the main forms. At first black, white and grays are sufficient to establish the design and to spotlight key action points. Discuss your design with the lighting manager at this point.

The careful use of lighting creates atmosphere

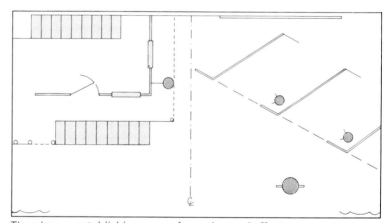

The plan — establishing space for acting and effect

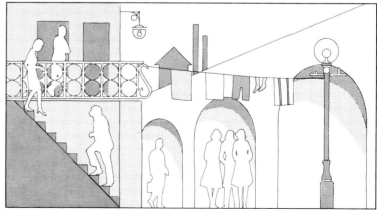

Actors give a setting its true scale and point of focus

General principles of design

Balance and composition

Balance is not a straightforward equal distribution of mass or form. It is a satisfying harmonious arrangement which can be achieved in many ways.

Nevertheless, symmetry (or the equal balance of mass) has its place in scene design based on the center stage line. Its use on stage can be severe and imposing and is best suited to architectural features: a cathedral nave, arches, pillars, castle gates etc. These structures draw the eye down into center stage. The severity may be softened by color, light and texture and the positioning of props.

Proscenium stage box sets are by their very nature restricting. By adding symmetry to a limiting frame you create a potentially boring stage against which any script must struggle.

Use a variety of flats to make the eye 'work'. Narrow flats, I or 2 feet (30-60 cm) wide can be inserted into the design to relieve the predictability of long, flat surfaces. These are not purely cosmetic. The extra space created provides room for properties like cabinets, bookcases and clocks without interfering with the movement of the cast.

Symmetry does not end in the use of horizontal and vertical lines. It can also apply when the general movement of line is circular.

This radial balance, though at first sight more interesting, can pose similar visual problems and limit acting movement.

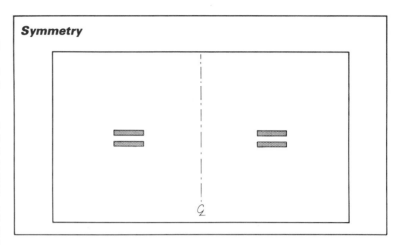

Symmetry

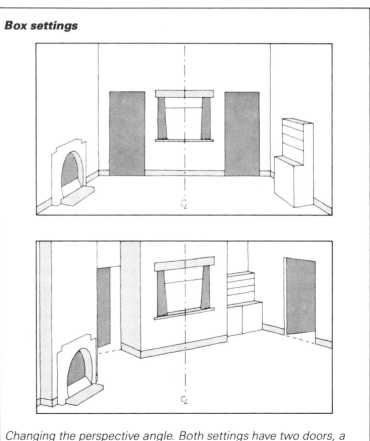

Box settings

Changing the perspective angle. Both settings have two doors, a window, fireplace and bookcase

The designer must balance form against space sensitively. The design elements of light, line, proportion and movement all contribute to this intuitive process. The scenic design should have a focal point but this must not conflict with the unassailable fact that the actor is obviously the center of attention.

The relationship of people to objects is important and often significant to the play (the balcony scene in *Romeo and Juliet* is a case in point). Scenery cannot make a production but it is a vital ingredient. It can add flavor and heighten the enjoyment of the 'dramatic' dish. Balance should therefore be subtle and changeable. Relate the set to the action. Transmit the atmosphere by a calculated use of design elements. A light, frothy play deserves a bright, pastel colored setting. Build in wide, thinly framed french windows overlooking a sunlit skycloth. Balance the window with a raised entrance so that actors can enter with a 'hop and a skip'! Add strongly colored flowers as an additional point of focus.

If a setting is simple, make it look clean and functional. Experiment with geometrical shapes and carry this concept through into properties. Use primary colors for drapes and coverings.

A threatening play needs an intimidating claustrophobic setting, heavy arches, bulky pillars and small doorways. Rigid ironwork and somber colors can be balanced by a small source of light from a high window or a crack of light under a door or through a heavy curtain.

A severe setting

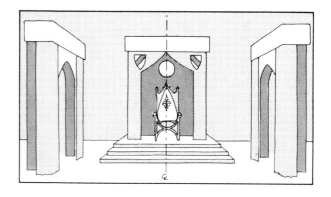

A severe setting relieved by subtle lighting from stage left

A radial setting

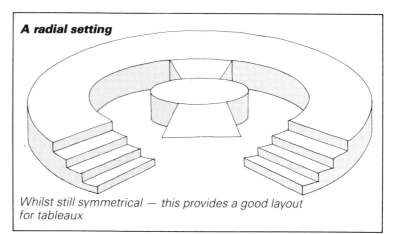

Whilst still symmetrical — this provides a good layout for tableaux

Using perspective

When a stage design needs to be realistic, the designer must understand the basic rules of linear perspective or foreshortening. Properly applied, these rules will give the illusion of distance and space to what otherwise might be a shallow stage. They also enable the designer to create a three-dimensional effect from two-dimensional cloth.

Horizon or eye level

The horizon or eye level is the apparent line which divides the land or sea from the sky. It will vary depending upon the position of the observer. The sailor in the crows-nest will have a more distant horizon than the captain on the deck of the ship.

The designer's first task is to establish the horizon or eye level on the back-cloth or back wall. This can vary according to the demands of the play and the shape of the theater.

If the auditorium is flat and the seating is below the stage floor level the audience will be looking upwards, so fix the eye level some 4 to 6 feet (1 to 2m) above the stage floor. If the seating is raked you must compromise. Sit in the center of the auditorium and look straight ahead. Ask a colleague to mark your selected eye level.

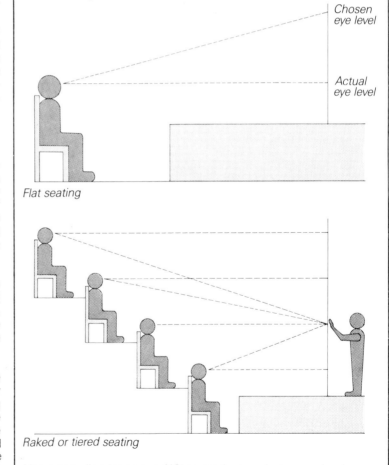

Establishing a horizon

Chosen
eye level

Actual
eye level

Flat seating

Raked or tiered seating

Use a snap line (see page 113) to mark your chosen eye level which must be parallel to the stage floor.

Parallel lines

Parallel lines when leading away to the horizon appear to converge until they meet at a vanishing point. This rule applies to horizontal parallel planes as well as vertical ones. Vertical lines remain vertical throughout.

Railway tracks and telegraph poles illustrate this principle well.

In a landscape there are effectively two vanishing points — to left and right of your vision.

By using the second vanishing point, most of the required distance effects can be achieved.

Additional vanishing points may be added to break up the rigidity of the scene. They must be on the same eye level and the principle of parallel lines still holds good.

To apply these basic techniques, draw a scaled, squared front elevation of the proscenium opening, allowing a generous border.

Draw in your projected eye level. Mark your on stage vanishing point as far to one side as possible. Mark your second vanishing point along the eye level, well outside the proscenium edge.

Mark on this plan your basic design, remembering your perspective principles of parallel lines converging to a vanishing point and vertical lines remaining perpendicular. When you have established your projected main outlines, note the distances and angles and reproduce them on the stage surface to be painted.

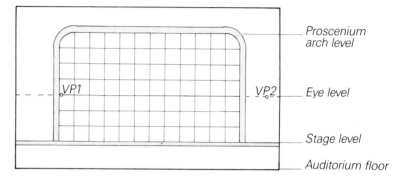

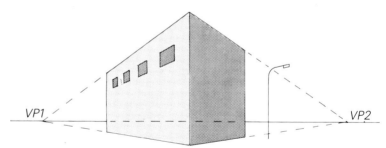

Low eye level — gives an extra feeling of height to the set.

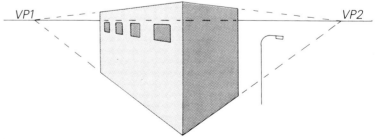

High eye level — gives the audience the impression of looking down on the set from a high vantage point.

Using perspective

Three-dimensional perspective

This is a most difficult aspect of designing and painting scenery. Although one could embark upon time-consuming full graphic lay-out, the perspective technique should guide rather than control a design. It is unwise to impose too severe a perspective line on a small stage, but it is useful on occasions to provide extra depth.

On small stages the suggestion of depth can be reinforced by the addition of masking pieces over the parallel edges of a flat.

1 *The eye level or horizon painted on the back-cloth is constant, as are the vanishing points. However, if the scene to be depicted is busy with flats at different angles on the stage, the vanishing points may move along the horizon or eye level*

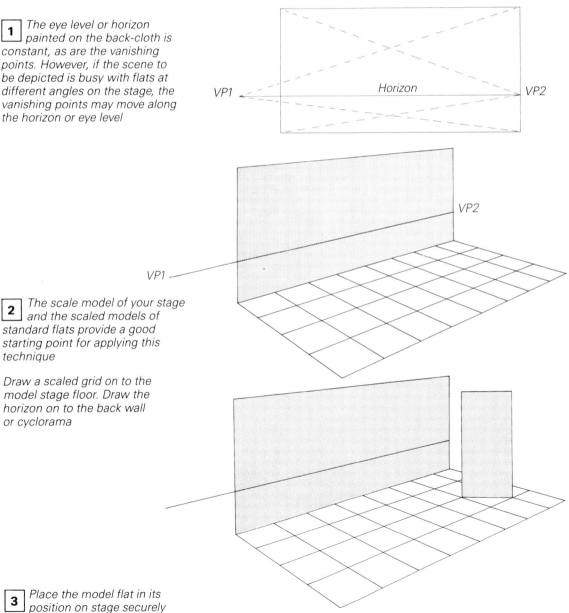

2 *The scale model of your stage and the scaled models of standard flats provide a good starting point for applying this technique*

Draw a scaled grid on to the model stage floor. Draw the horizon on to the back wall or cyclorama

3 *Place the model flat in its position on stage securely*

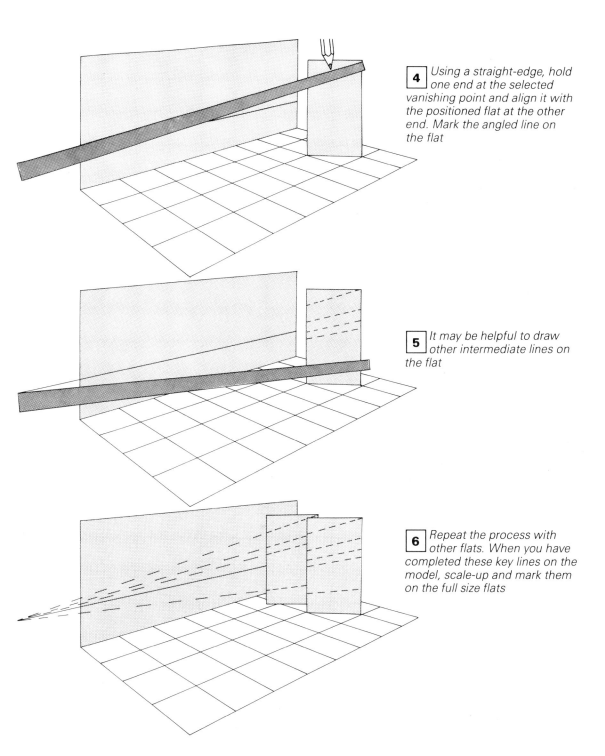

4 Using a straight-edge, hold one end at the selected vanishing point and align it with the positioned flat at the other end. Mark the angled line on the flat

5 It may be helpful to draw other intermediate lines on the flat

6 Repeat the process with other flats. When you have completed these key lines on the model, scale-up and mark them on the full size flats

Using perspective

Exaggerating perspective

Edges on a horizontal plane will require masking to reinforce the perspective line of roof lines, upper windows and the tops of walls. Remember not to overdo the severity of the perspective. The design will lose credibility if there is an entrance so far up stage that the actor appears as a giant, only to shrink to normal size as he advances down stage.

Shaped hardboard fillet

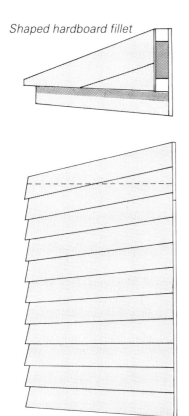

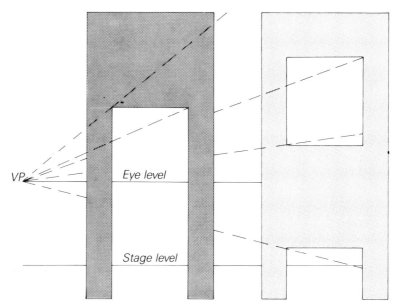

Lines of brickwork, layers of weatherboarding and roof lines painted along the perspective guidelines add considerable realism to the illusion. The width of the bricks or planks will foreshorten as they 'recede'.

If you plan operating doors or windows add fillets of hardboard to the parallel edges. The vertical edges will remain vertical. To accentuate the roof line, add a shaped triangle of hardboard to the top of the flat if the stage height allows. Nail a reinforcing batten to the up stage side and attach it to the parent flat. Mask the butted joint before painting.

If your design features an aisle or canopy, the up stage dimensions will reduce in actual measurement as this recedes and increase as it advances. The same reduction applies to reveals and returns.

It is risky to attempt these illusions with a trucked unit as its position on stage will vary and the perspective will not always be true.

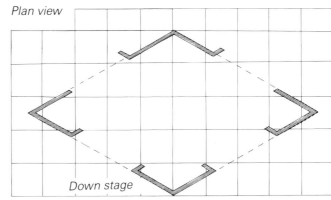
Plan view

Down stage

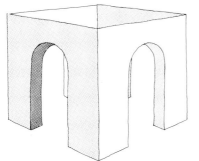
Constructed unit

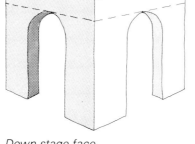
Down stage face

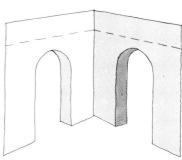
Up stage face

Atmospheric perspective

Perspective lines may be accentuated for dramatic effect. A high vertical sight-line is an advantage here and is most effective when used in conjunction with a thrust stage setting. The very line of the thrust creates an illusion of depth which can be exaggerated by the fillet methods described above. Establish the horizon and bring the vanishing points closer together — avoid the center-line position and you will create an interesting assymmetrical design

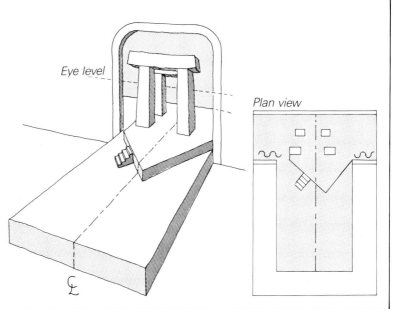
Eye level

Plan view

Scale drawings

Using symbols

The director, stage manager and property mistress or master will need some guidance in planning and plotting the set you have devised. In addition to the stage model (see page 46) it is advisable to draw out a plan: a simplified map of the stage deck.

If there are to be permanent features on stage such as doors, stairways, stanchions, a proscenium arch or curtain line, measure and mark these on the plan.

Very basic line drawings are quite adequate, using conventional symbols, understood by all, and the minimum of words.

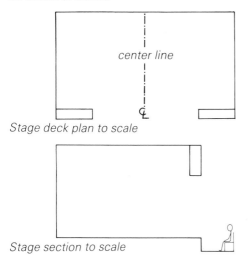

Stage deck plan to scale

Stage section to scale

Cloths

Curtains, (tabs) and traverse curtains

Fixed cyclorama/sky-cloth or fixed back-cloth

Rolled back-cloth or olio

Border

Gauze

All items positioned or stored above stage are shown by dashed lines

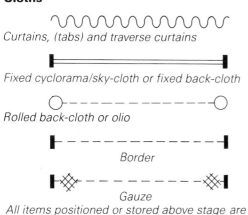

Different levels

Different levels created by rostra, platforms or trucks are drawn to scale with diagonal lines to distinguish them from tables and so on.

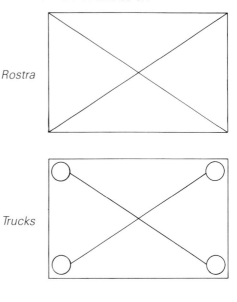

Rostra

Trucks

Steps, stairways and ramps

These are drawn with a directional arrow, the word 'UP', and measurements of height above stage level.

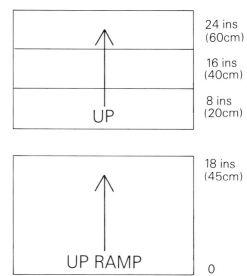

UP	24 ins (60cm)
	16 ins (40cm)
	8 ins (20cm)
UP RAMP	18 ins (45cm)
	0

Ground rows

The simple two-dimensional cut-out is marked as a line with support but no capping (see Flats below)

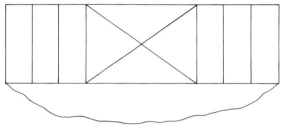

Plan view

Three-dimensional ground rows are drawn in outline with additional information symbolized

Flats

A line drawn to scale and capped denotes a single, plain flat.

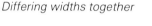

Plain flat

Differing widths together

Door flat

Window

Fireplace

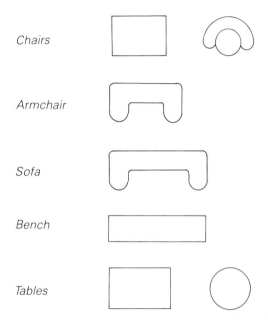

Bay window

Plain flat with cut-out profile (the cut-out is not capped)

Properties

These are symbolized by their approximate shape and size.

Chairs

Armchair

Sofa

Bench

Tables

Where hinges or pivots are used in scene changing, mark and name the pivot point. Indicate the start by a solid line, direction by arrow and the new position with a dotted line.

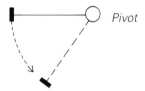

Pivot

Similarly with tabs or traverse curtains, draw in the symbol for their fixed position and a dotted line to show their position in following scenes.

You may wish to use different colored pencils or ink to clarify scene changes and property movement.

Variations to these symbols may be used but they must be commonly understood by all members of the production team.

Scale drawings

These drawings explain how you can pass on helpful and accurate information to the stage manager. They describe the angle and type of flat required. They show the on-stage view clearly and are also a guide to atmosphere and space. The stage manager can assess the amount of storage space available backstage and can plan his change priorities list.

Before building the set, mark out the proposed set lines in colored adhesive tape on the stage. Use a different color tape for subsequent scene layouts. The scene erectors can then proceed quickly.

The position of props can also be marked in this way.

Interior setting

Stock units

four 4 ft (120 cm) door flats
one 6 ft (180 cm) french window
two 4 ft (120 cm) plain flats
four 1 ft (30 cm) plain flats
one 2 ft (60 cm) plain flat
one 3 ft (90 cm) plain flat

one 6 x 4 ft (180 x 120 cm) rostra 3 ft (90 cm) high

2 sets steps 3 ft (90 cm) high

I painted back-cloth behind small window
I cut-out profile
I masking flat behind door

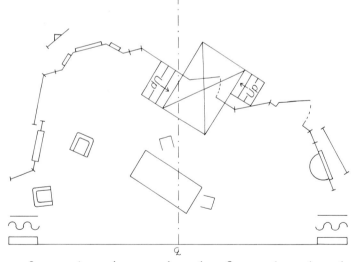

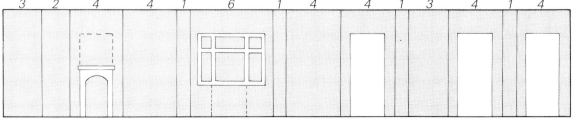

An area not sufficiently dealt with by the ground plan symbol layout is the fly area or stage ceiling. This is the home of borders, cut cloths and rollers as well as any tripped unit of scenery. In addition to the set plan illustrated, the stage manager will require a side elevation of the stage, listing the position and name of the flown units, i.e. no: I stalactites, no: 2 forest cut cloth, no: 3 village roller, etc. He also needs a chart clearly numbering and naming the stage ropes and cleats so that other members of the stage crew can operate the fly in a crisis. When the stage manager has all the scene drawings he can organize the schedule of working priorities and changes.

Stock units

four 10ft (3 m) door flats
two standard doors
three 2ft (60 cm) plain flats

two 6 x 3ft (180 x 90 cm) rostra 2 ft (60 cm) high

one 6 x 4ft (180 x 120 cm) rostra 4 ft (120 cm) high

two 2ft (60 cm) rising ramps
one 4ft (120 cm) rising ramp
one stage width gauze
one stage width back-cloth
two various cut profiles (trees)
two leaf borders. Stage width

Exterior setting

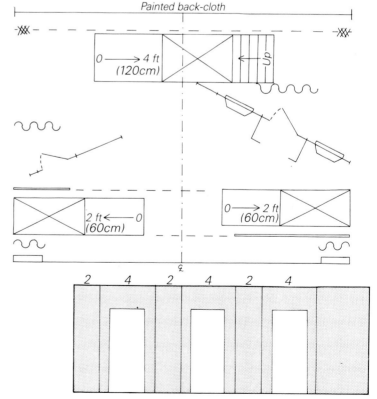

Painted back-cloth

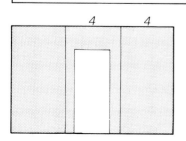

Controlling sight-lines

Proscenium stage

The set designer has a great deal of influence over the shape of the 'picture' presented to the audience. The mood and movement of a play does not always require the full stage width and height. Make use of wing flats, leg curtains, borders and a sky-cloth, as well as teasers and tormentors to mask your stage.

Firstly, establish your basic sight-lines. Draw an accurate side elevation of the stage. Include in the scale drawing the measurement from the stage front to the front row of seating. Draw a simple figure seated in the front row and projected dotted sight-lines through the proscenium arch. This will indicate the maximum vision.

If you possess a cyclorama or permanent sky-cloth, position it away from the back wall allowing sufficient space for passage.
The bottom edges of borders are generally level with the proscenium arch. Project a dotted line on to your side elevation. The deeper the stage, the more borders will be needed. You will find that they are placed further apart as they recede into the stage area.

Make every effort to increase the height on stage and avoid an untidy stage ceiling. That front row patron naturally looks upwards and is close enough to see the 'joins'. An untidy clutter of lighting battens, odd ropes and pulleys does disturb the eye.

There are occasions when a smaller stage area can be an advantage, especially when the dialogue is all important. It is possible to reduce the dimensions of the stage arch by using teasers and tormentors.

Tormentors

Flats are positioned behind the curtain line. These will narrow the width of the proscenium arch.

Teasers

These can be flats, or a curtain border which is lowered to the selected height and set in front of the tormentors. This system will radically alter the established sight-lines, and borders and wing flats will require adjustment. However, it does have the added benefit of increasing the wing and backstage space.

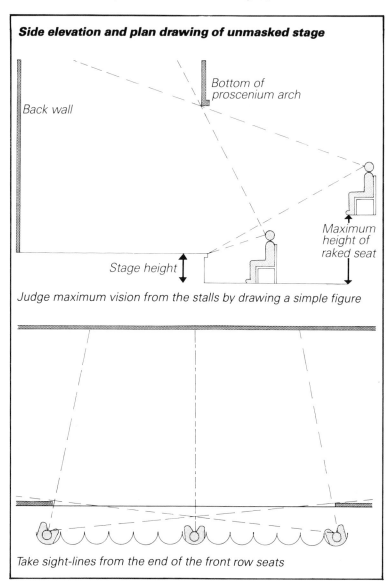

Side elevation and plan drawing of unmasked stage

Back wall

Bottom of proscenium arch

Stage height

Maximum height of raked seat

Judge maximum vision from the stalls by drawing a simple figure

Take sight-lines from the end of the front row seats

Take care to arrange scenery and action in such a manner that critical points of the play are not missed by any of the audience. With a low, narrow proscenium, it may be possible to extend the stage apron and bring the action forward into the auditorium to reduce dead space. The stage sight-lines will change slightly but the space for acting will be improved. This arrangement allows you to dress the extended apron permanently while still retaining the curtain 'punctuation'. Of course, this means that some of the stalls seating, along with the ticket income, will be reduced.

Thrust stage

In thrust stage productions controlled sight-lines are much less important. The key seated sight-lines are those nearest the main stage entrances. Simple adjustment of main curtains or traverse curtains will usually suffice. The audience needs protection only from the chaos of cast assembly and movement of stage machinery. It will enjoy the heightened involvement of increased proximity with the performers.

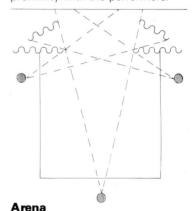

Arena

Again, direct the audience's attention away from the stage mechanics. Loose or errant power cables or glimpses of untidy dressing space can destroy the atmosphere — Here as nowhere else, the audience must look the other way!

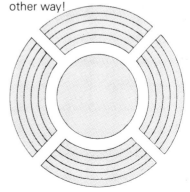

Position of borders

Tormentor

3 ft

Back wall

Cyclorama

If space allows set the cyclorama 3 feet (90 cm) from back wall

Cyclorama　　*3 ft (90cm)*

Flats and borders should be the same height for easy adjustment

Materials and tools for design and modeling

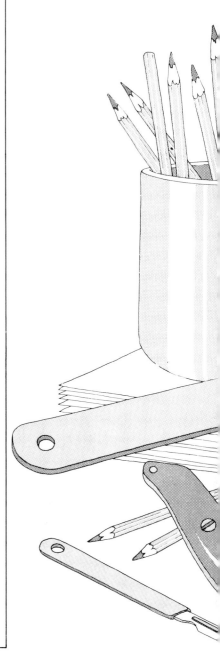

Design

Materials	Use
Felt tip and day-glo pens	Preliminary sketching and coloring
Pencils	As required. For scale drawings use harder (3H)
China pencils	For preliminary planning
Stanley knife	For accurate cutting
Scalpel (designer's)	For detailed cutting
Gummed paper tape	For model making
Cellophane tape	For securing
Masking tape	Adhesive and can be written on
Tracing paper	
Cartridge/drawing paper	For sketching
Cardboard — various thicknesses	Model making and some prop-making
Plastic sheeting	For protecting surfaces and transparency — windows, water, etc
Erasers	For mistakes!
Rubber gum	Easily removable glue
Sable brushes	For model painting
Hogshair brushes	General props painting
Rulers and straight-edges	
Compasses Set squares	

Modeling

Plasticine	For indicating props
Clay	Prepacked and ready to use from art stores — slow drying
Papier mâché	Best employed in prop-making — rather messy in a design context
Cellulose filler	Good for denoting texture on walls etc.
Plastic cardboard	Brittle when cold, malleable when warm
Modeling tools	Used for working with clay

Stage model making

After an initial discussion with the director, it is of considerable help to construct a model, no matter how basic your design layout is at this time. Your subsequent discussions with the stage manager, property and lighting teams will be much more relevant.

Use hardboard or thin plywood as a baseboard. Cover the surface with white cardboard and glue it down. Choose a sensible scale — 1 inch to 1 foot (25 to 300mm) is convenient — and boldly mark out the ground plan of your stage, the proscenium, the curtained setting line, the stage center line, back wall and cyclorama so that the baseboard and its stage plan may be used more than once.

Next, cover the whole board with a sturdy transparent plastic sheet. All subsequent markings made with a china pencil are then easily removed.

Box sets

Transcribe your original sketches into a plan on the baseboard, outlining the flat arrangements using design symbols. Applying the same scale of 1 inch to 1 foot (25 to 300mm) draw on the separate faces and features of the setting. When this has been completed, paint the general color values on to the drawing.

This sequence will avoid the curling of small pieces of cardboard when water-based paint is used. If you need to fold some sections, score lightly on the reverse side along the line of the fold. The separate sections may be joined together by gummed paper or by tabs. If one or more sections need to be moved or adjusted, make them self standing by adding a rear leg or bracket. If all sections can be supported in this way there is no need to glue the setting on to the baseboard until the mechanics have been fully discussed with the stage manager, and any movement problems solved.

Rostras and props can be made in simplified dimensions or matchboxes, shoeboxes and so on used in their place.

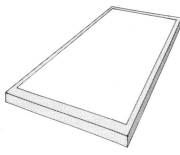

1 *Make a baseboard from thin ply covered with cardboard using a rubber adhesive*

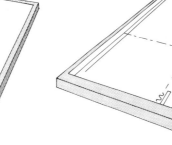

2 *Draw in your stage lines boldly, using a sensible scale with a marker pen*

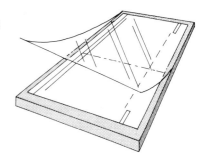

3 *A layer of plastic allows you to alter china pencil marks made in the early stages*

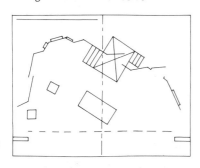

4 *Use the symbols on page 39 to show the main setting features. Keep them simple*

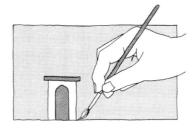

5 *Paint the general color levels on to the drawing before attempting to cut any out*

6 *To fold sections, score lightly on the reverse side first, and gently bend against a ruler*

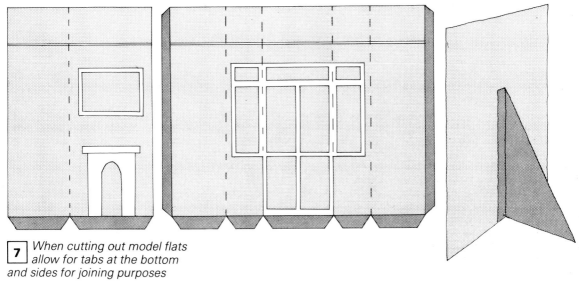

7 When cutting out model flats allow for tabs at the bottom and sides for joining purposes

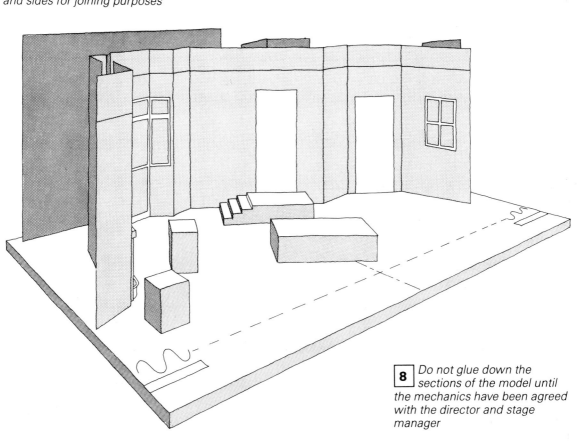

8 Do not glue down the sections of the model until the mechanics have been agreed with the director and stage manager

Constructing the set

After all the sketching, exploratory discussions and conferences are over and the designs approved, the construction of the setting will present logistical problems. The more complicated the set, the greater the pressure placed upon the construction team. Time, materials, manpower and movement must each be dovetailed to get the scenery to the stage on time.

It is a fortunate drama society which has a large number of people involved in each department. It is not uncommon for stage carpenters to be 'bit' players, stage painters, wardrobe mistresses, and chorus singers. Encourage the actors to attend the set building sessions, to do the multiplicity of small, unskilled tasks which together can represent a brake on progress. Scene painting, for instance, involves not only skilled illusionary detail but sometimes a vast acreage of simple one-color application. Flat making, although assigned to the specialist at the construction stage, will later require nailing or gluing.

The practical involvement of the whole membership also makes for a more harmonious group.

Building specific 'one-off' units is best left to the most skilled and experienced of the construction team. Give these tasks priority and calculate the time-scale required to complete them. Critical Path Planning, though sounding a slightly pompous title, is the technical expression for getting the priorities right. It works well in stage construction. Set stringent targets at each session and strive to achieve them. The stage manager must estimate and obtain the quantities of any extra material at the beginning of the construction process. 'For the want of a nail the shoe was lost . . .!'

As the various units of the set are completed and painted, mark them off on the stage plan and store them carefully. Although many of these units are larger than life, they are more fragile and just as awkward to handle. The backstage crew are most adept at handling these sets but the transfer of all scenery from store to theater may need coordinated extra hands from the group membership.

However detailed and thorough the designer's plans may be, the peculiarities of the venue may make it necessary for on stage adjustments to be made. Extra stage weights, additional masking by flat or curtain, last minute repairs or painting may be needed. Be prepared.

The terms of your tenure will dictate the place and timing of your construction. The flow chart of progress on page 27 will help you to establish a sensible timetable.

Basic equipment

The variety of tools necessary to stock a stage workshop has lessened since the development of electric hand tools. The versatility of these now seems to know few bounds. Although many of the stage team will have personal tool boxes, your society would be well advised to invest in a selection of basic tools which remain permanently in the workshop. The stage manager should have the responsibility for keeping track of and maintaining the efficiency of the tools.

Work surfaces and trestles as well as the portable work bench are best sited along one side of the workshop where they provide a safe home for dangerous tools and allow free access along the length of the workshop. Stores often have heavy old furniture which can easily be converted. A scenery dock constructed in 2 x 1 inch (50 x 25mm) timber is a very good investment. If this can be built to allow vertical storage of flats so much the better. The gradual addition of flat furniture, cleats, eyelets etc. can, if the flat is carelessly stored, cause irritating damage to the canvas surfaces.

Endeavor to store screws and nails in an orderly fashion. Washed out truncated plastic detergent bottles, especially those with preformed handles, make convenient storage packs which sit comfortably on shelves. You may find it useful to store the most frequently used nails and screws on a wheeled trolley.

Encourage all of your group members to be hoarders. Hinges, door-handles, locks, brackets and the like are invaluable. Bolts and nuts of all shapes and sizes or other items of ironmongery which have, over the years, become progressively more expensive to buy, should also be collected.

It is a temptation to keep odd pieces of timber and strangely shaped hardboard in the belief that this is an economy in materials and time. Don't be fooled. By all means keep a tea chest or barrel in which lengths of reasonable timber may be stored vertically. Then you can see what you have at a glance. Throw away those 'may be useful' scraps.

Purchase a variety of step ladders. The 'A' framed type with a platform is most useful as on flimsy flat settings much of the work is at a height where both hands are needed. Working above one's eye level is doubly fatiguing and you must feel secure.

A supply of different colored adhesive tape is useful for marking stage scenery and the stage deck to indicate line and changes of position of scenic units.

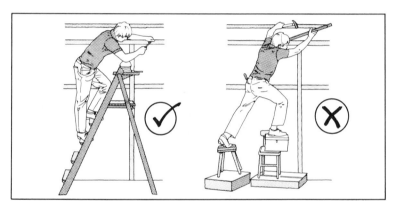

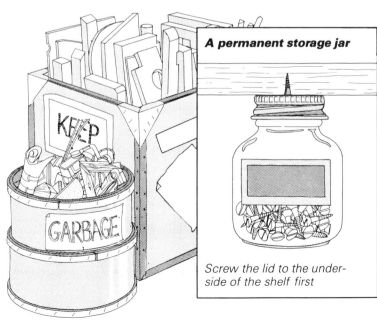

A permanent storage jar

Screw the lid to the underside of the shelf first

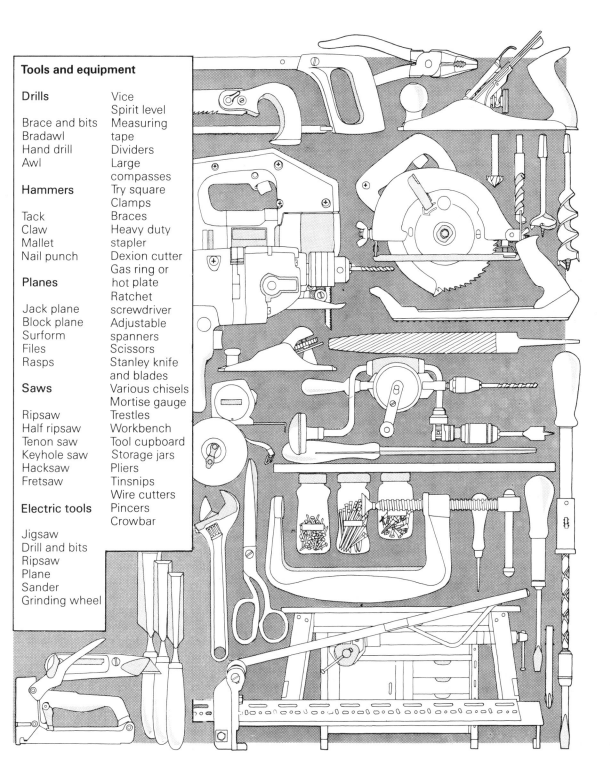

Tools and equipment

Drills

Brace and bits
Bradawl
Hand drill
Awl

Hammers

Tack
Claw
Mallet
Nail punch

Planes

Jack plane
Block plane
Surform
Files
Rasps

Saws

Ripsaw
Half ripsaw
Tenon saw
Keyhole saw
Hacksaw
Fretsaw

Electric tools

Jigsaw
Drill and bits
Ripsaw
Plane
Sander
Grinding wheel

Vice
Spirit level
Measuring tape
Dividers
Large compasses
Try square
Clamps
Braces
Heavy duty stapler
Dexion cutter
Gas ring or hot plate
Ratchet screwdriver
Adjustable spanners
Scissors
Stanley knife and blades
Various chisels
Mortise gauge
Trestles
Workbench
Tool cupboard
Storage jars
Pliers
Tinsnips
Wire cutters
Pincers
Crowbar

Materials for set construction

Scenic canvas and alternative coverings

Flax canvas — Available in 3 x 6 ft (90 x 180 cm) widths. Lightweight, tightly woven material ideal for covering flats, back-cloths or cyclorama. It does not shrink excessively.

Cotton duck — Similar material to flax canvas but more expensive.

Sack cloth/hessian — Unlike flax canvas both the fiber and the weave are loose. Shrinking after sizing is severe. If it is too tightly drawn, it can warp the flat. Tends to unravel at the edges. It has a shorter life than canvas. Buy in 6 ft (180 cm) and 12 ft (3½ m) widths.

Cardboard — Large packing cases are made in robust reinforced cardboard. Cuts easily with a stanley knife. It must be approved before use by the local fire officer.

Scrim/gauze — Very light and widely meshed to allow light to pass through it effectively.

Muslin — A soft and fluffy material useful in diffusing light when stretched over a timber frame.

Timber

Pine — 2 x 1 ft (60 x 30 cm) and 3 x 1 ft (90 x 30 cm) planed timber battens are most used and most flats are made in this sized wood. More substantial timbers are required for load-bearing units, rostra, stairs, supports.

Plywood — Increasingly expensive, available in many sizes and is a reliable floor covering.

Composition board — Made by compressing small pieces of wastewood together. Has no impact strength and is unsuitable for flooring but easily shaped for shelving unit tops etc.

Blockboard or particle board — A timber 'sandwich' with impact strength. An alternative to using plywood.

Hardboard — Now more readily available in thinner gauge. Makes the flat much heavier, but is versatile and robust enough to need only the most basic of support e.g. ground rows.

Ensure that all materials are fireproofed before use.

Assorted ironmongery

Screws 1 to 3 in (25 to 75 mm) countersunk.

Nails oval 1 to 2½ inches (25 to 65 mm)
Nails round 1 to 2½ inches (25 to 65 mm).

Nuts and bolts of all types
Pins, panel, hardboard pins
Tacks for canvas surfaces
Ball catches, hooks and eyes
hasp and staples.

Hinges of all sizes. Large hinges are particularly useful for scenery in small stage situations, also old door catches.

Brackets, mild steel angles, rawlplugs, door handles, latches, yale locks, cleats, pulleys, sheaves, cable and wire.

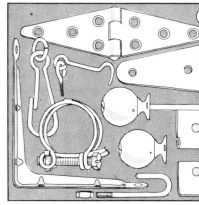

Flats

Simple framework

A flat is a rectangular area of canvas, reinforced by a timber frame upon which scenes are painted. The flat is the traditional unit of stage scenery, which has replaced the wall or curtain of open air presentations. Its purpose is simple: to mask the backstage and wing section of the stage, while at the same time creating illusion and atmosphere. It remains the most effective and practical method of stage decoration.

Avoid making all flats to the same dimensions. Wing flats need be no wider than 3 feet (90 cm), and no stage should require more than three on each side to mask backstage activity effectively.

The wooden framework consists of a rail, stile toggle rail and brace. The corner joints must be strongly made, preferably with mortise and tenon joints — the mortise into the rail and the tenon into the stile. The toggle rail requires only a halving joint. If the corners are joined in a more simple manner you should reinforce these with triangular plywood plates. The flat must be rectangular to avoid difficult gaps when butting one flat to another.

Interior scenes in a play require box sets (see page 30) and a variety of widths of flat enables the designer to create a more interesting set. Their construction remains the same.

The basic units needed include a selection of plain flats and a number of door flats. Using them properly offers considerable scope within the setting. The door flat may, by use of filler flats, be converted to house windows,

A standard flat

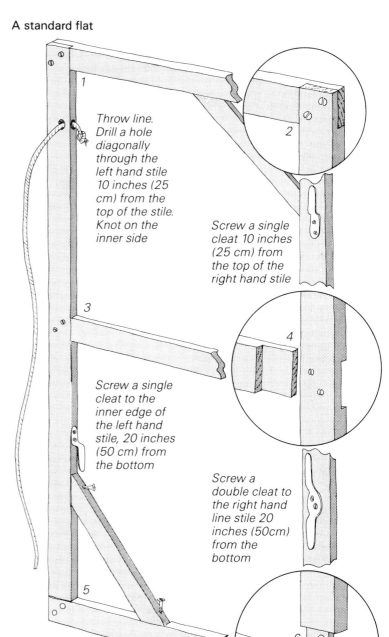

Throw line. Drill a hole diagonally through the left hand stile 10 inches (25 cm) from the top of the stile. Knot on the inner side

Screw a single cleat 10 inches (25 cm) from the top of the right hand stile

Screw a single cleat to the inner edge of the left hand stile, 20 inches (50 cm) from the bottom

Screw a double cleat to the right hand line stile 20 inches (50cm) from the bottom

Joints 1,2,3 and 4 are halving joints

Joints 5 and 6 are hidden mortise and tenon braces glued and screwed

cupboards, etc. but when employed as a straightforward door it must, of course, be able to withstand movement. As all flats are connected one to another the lateral stresses and occasional violent impact has to be absorbed by the construction of the flat itself. The dramatic exit of a spurned lover is ruined if, as he slams the door, the whole set shivers and shakes!

Construct the door flat in more sustantial timber. 2 inches x 2 inches (50 mm x 50 mm) will suffice. It does increase the overall weight but helps stability considerably. The addition of a metal plate across the feet of the flat is also helpful particularly if you can screw it down into the stage floor. Screw the stage brace eye some 5 feet (152 cm) from the floor on the outer stiles.

A wide gap between flats can be filled by placing two boards against the flat edges and bracing at the top and bottom by horizontal timbers. This is a useful device if your design calls for peculiarly shaped windows or alcoves.

All joints should be glued and screwed. Cleats and throw lines should be fixed after the flat has been covered. Ensure that all corners are accurately 90 degrees.

Temporary time-saving fastenings and joints can be found on page 81 but should not replace the traditional methods.

Note When building flats to suit your stage, refer to your original side elevation drawing of the stage (see page 42) to determine the minimum height.

A door flat

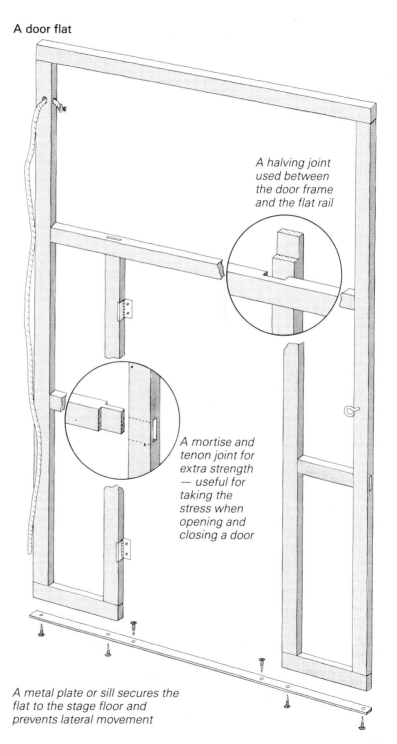

A halving joint used between the door frame and the flat rail

A mortise and tenon joint for extra strength — useful for taking the stress when opening and closing a door

A metal plate or sill secures the flat to the stage floor and prevents lateral movement

Flats

Covering the frame

Scenery flats need a tautly drawn covering. An artist working in oils first stretches his canvas over loosely joined stretchers and after sizing and priming, tightens wedges to enlarge the timber frame evenly prior to painting. The stage painter does not have this facility and consequently must take greater care when covering the framework of the flat.

A variety of material is available for covering flats. The most efficient is canvas. It is also the most expensive. Scenic canvas in the form of either cotton or flax duck can be purchased already. fireproofed from established suppliers. When stretched it produces a fine tight surface. It is also light and makes scene shifting an easy task.

Hessian or sack cloth is an alternative. The tightly woven variety can be used to cover flats inexpensively but even after several coats of paint, the surface retains a texture which does not marry well with canvas. However it is a very useful lightweight, multi-purpose material providing it is fireproofed before use on stage.

A hardboard or plywood covering adds considerable weight and rigidity to a frame. It makes an ideal host flat for hinges and means that convenient shapes can be cut out. More effort is involved for the stage hands and scene erectors of course!

Hardboard comes in different thicknesses, use the thinnest available. These generally measure 8 x 4 feet (243 x 121 cm) and so more than one sheet will be needed for larger flats. To make certain that the edges are well

secured, cut the hardboard to meet on a rail. Glue and tack the sheets and butt the two pieces of hardboard neatly. Whatever gap remains between them can be filled quite easily with a proprietory cellulose filler.

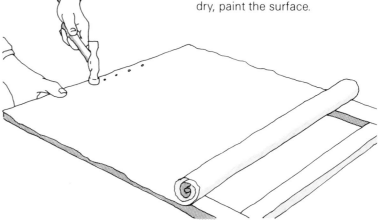

1 Cut the canvas 1 inch (25mm) longer and 1 inch wider than your frame. Support the frame on tables and make sure that it does not sag. Working

The shiny surface of hardboard is best rubbed down with glass paper before sizing and priming. If another material is used, ensure that it is fireproofed.

Fix on flat cleats and a throw rope, and when the flat is thoroughly dry, paint the surface.

always from the center of the rail, nail a line of tacks 1 inch (25 mm) apart, 2 inches (50 mm) from the outer edge of the bottom rail

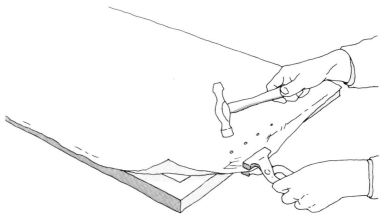

2 With one end securely and evenly tacked, stretch the canvas over the edge of the top rail. A pair of canvas pliers is useful for this task. Tack as with

the bottom rail. Repeat this procedure on the stiles, remembering to work outwards from the center

3 Lift back the edge of the secured canvas and apply glue to the timber beneath

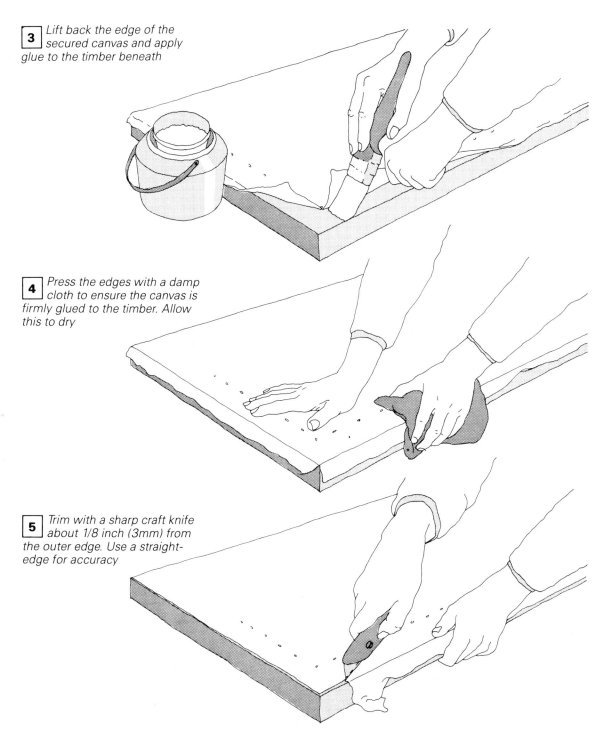

4 Press the edges with a damp cloth to ensure the canvas is firmly glued to the timber. Allow this to dry

5 Trim with a sharp craft knife about 1/8 inch (3mm) from the outer edge. Use a straight-edge for accuracy

Flats

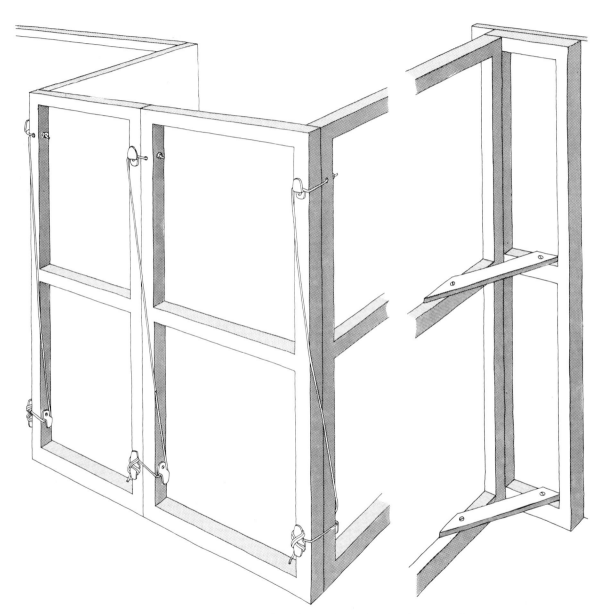

Securing and bracing

The throw line attached to the left hand stile (of each flat) is flicked over the cleat on the right hand stile of its neighbour. This is pulled tight to bring the flats together, passed under the cleat fixed on the inner edge of the left hand stile and finally tied off on the double cleat. This sequence is made easier if all cleats and throw lines are the same distance from the top and bottom of each flat.

Make sure pillars, trees and other free-standing objects are properly secure and do not tremble at the mere brush of a gown!

Nail or screw bracing timber at the toggle rail level and base rail just in excess of the tension required. The set should then remain firm.

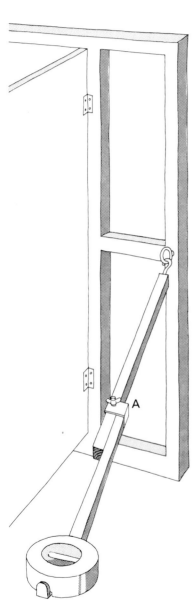

Alternative bracing

1 Angle brackets should be set below eye level.

2 The batten with screwed on 'blade' fits into a folded metal bracket below the top rail.

3 The simplest system which, if used too often, destroys the top rail timber.

4 Nails inside the stile can be adjusted to increase tautness.

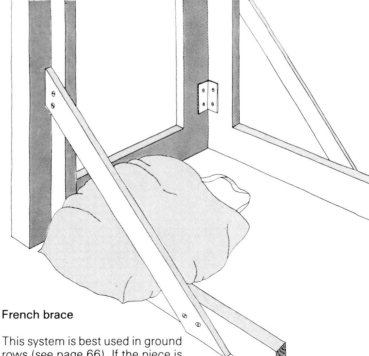

Braces and weights

A stage brace is adjustable (See the wing bolt **A** illustrated above.) This provides a counter pressure in a lateral direction and can be purchased ready made. If space is short use one of the following.

French brace

This system is best used in ground rows (see page 66). If the piece is above 3½ feet (106 cm) use a weight or sandbag (with a carrying loop sewn in). Fit hinges on the inside face so that the brace folds into the unit for easy handling and storage.

Filler flats

This is a simple flat built to the standard door width. The height can vary according to the requirements of the scene.

It is fixed to the door flat frame by hinges in which the pin has been replaced by a nail. Screw the hinge plates at the outer edges of the timber and tether the nail to the filler flat so that it can be pulled out without undue effort. These detachable hinges can be employed in all stage construction where changes need to be quick and simple.

The basic construction resembles that of the standard flat except that the inner stiles are jointed into the toggle rail and the bottom timbers are secured to a sill. This gives the flat the rigidity necessary when working doors or window frames exert a lateral stress.

The throw line and securing cleats are attached in the same manner as for the standard flat.

Box sets or permanent settings require an adequate supply of door flats. These are used not only as doors but also for windows, fireplaces, bookcases or alcoves, and give flexibility to the designer.

Interior windows are much more convincing if they appear to be recessed into the wall. The depth of this recess also adds an illusion of solidity to a setting. The window frame itself must fit inside the door flat opening. Its length will determine the height of the filler flat.

The nail is easily withdrawn from each hinge, making the addition and removal of the filler flat quick and efficient

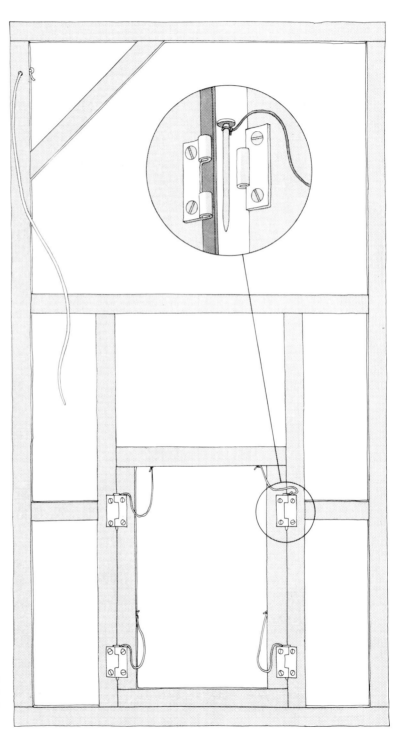

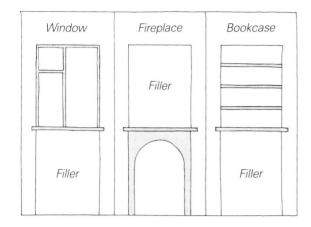

Window	Fireplace	Bookcase
	Filler	
Filler		Filler

Built to the width of a standard door, the filler flat varies in height according to the shape and nature of the unit

Interior window

To add thickness to the wall, insert a filler flat and nail a sill on to the top of this. If the sill exceeds 6 to 8 inches (20 cm) it will require a support bracket. Fix the window frame on to the sill and fill the side and top reveals with hardboard.

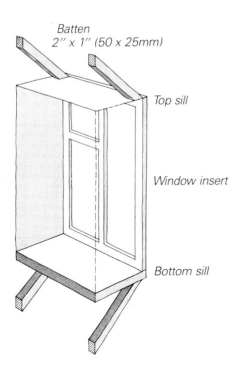

Batten
2" x 1" (50 x 25mm)

Top sill

Window insert

Bottom sill

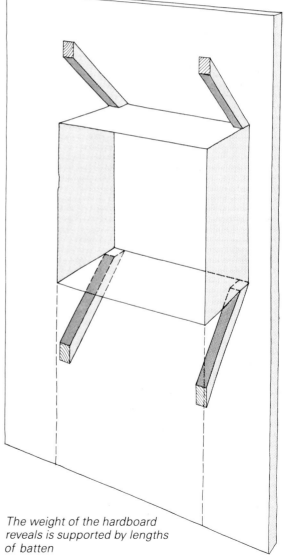

The weight of the hardboard reveals is supported by lengths of batten

Filler flats

Exterior windows

Moldings or architraves will disguise the gap between window and door opening. The addition of a sill to the top of the filler flat also helps to support the weight of the window frame.

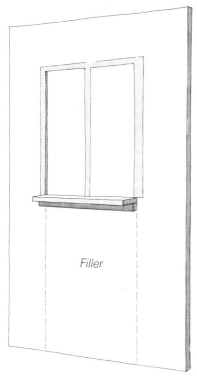

Filler

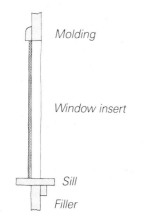

Molding

Window insert

Sill

Filler

Lattice windows

The lattice or leading effect can be achieved either by painting acrylic or oil paint on to plastic sheeting or plastic film or simply by using black tape at the off stage edge of the window frame. If the tape is adhesive, prevent it coming unstuck by sandwiching the tape ends between the hardboard reveal and a strip of cardboard or plywood. Make sure it is tightly fixed and straight.

For accuracy you can draw the lattice pattern on to a piece of white cardboard first. Placed behind the clear plastic it will act as a helpful design guide for tape or paint, and you will finish the job more quickly.

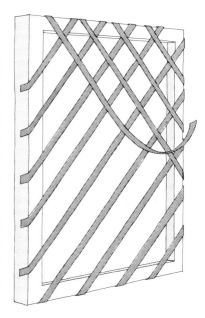

Apertures

Applying the same principle, use the filler to close the unwanted door space and construct the reveals necessary in hardboard. Do remember to mask the joints from powerful off-stage lighting

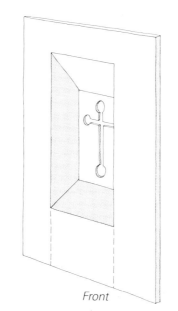

Front

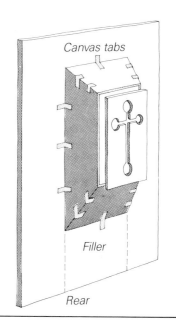

Canvas tabs

Filler

Rear

Church windows

The arched Gothic window used for church or castle windows, is quite straightforward to make. Cut the reveals from hardboard. If the arch curve is pronounced soak the hardboard in water first. If not, a restraining batten on the off side of the door opening held by canvas tape will be sufficient to maintain the shape of the arch and keep it in place.

The deeper the recess, the less accurate the window detail needs to be, but it is likely that the window will be a feature lit from the off stage side, so it must be a cleanly cut or a tidily made silhouette. If the recess is deep, the reveal support must be adequate to cover the reveal joints with masking tape to prevent light seepage. A slight gap could easily destroy the illusion.

 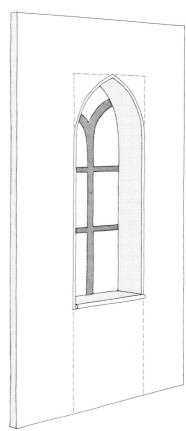

The weight of the reveal and sill can be supported by legs made from 2'' x 1'' (50 x 25mm) batten

Stained glass windows

Tack and glue the plastic sheet or film tautly across the window aperture. Paint in the 'leading' from the back with acrylic or oil paint and create transparent color variations with tissue papers or odd pieces of lighting gel. Add more layers of tissue to deepen the color tone. Fix with contact adhesive along the 'leading'.

Do not over-complicate the window design. Dramatic effect is better achieved with color than line.

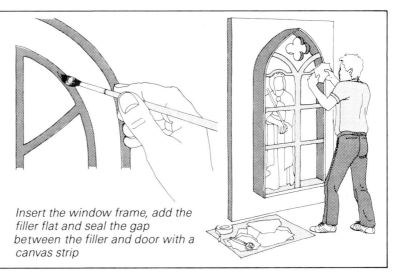

Insert the window frame, add the filler flat and seal the gap between the filler and door with a canvas strip

Filler flats

Fireplaces

In a box set, the fireplace is a recognized point of focus which can dominate the room. Because the eye is drawn to it, extra care must be taken in its construction. The more opulent the setting, the more imposing the structure of the fireplace needs to be.

Build a light framework, encased in hardboard on three sides, add on a return to suggest depth and paint this black. Decorate the fascia as appropriate.

Position the fireplace into the door flat and secure it with gate latches. Once the filler flat is in place glue small blocks of wood on to the underside of the mantel shelf so that it fits neatly within the box structure. Lay the mantel shelf on top of the fireplace.

Off stage, behind the fireplace, duplicate the light framework to house the 'burning fire' mechanics of electric bulb, logs, grate etc. This will protect it from accidental movements, and add to the illusion the depth of the chimney opening. Mask this area with cloth to prevent light and sound permeating on stage through the fireplace opening.

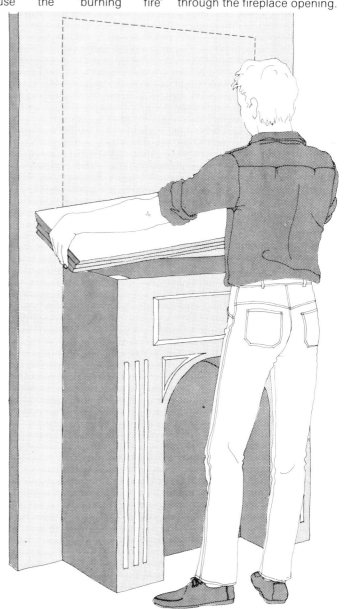

Bookcases or alcoves

As before, cut your filler flat, add
reveals, mask joints and then add
sheeting. This shelving can be
non-load bearing if you are using it
purely for display. To create a
deeper alcove make the
shadowed painted area more
dense and if the flat is well up
stage, you can re-draw the interior
perspective line. If it is not required
elsewhere, you could use the door
as the back of the alcove.

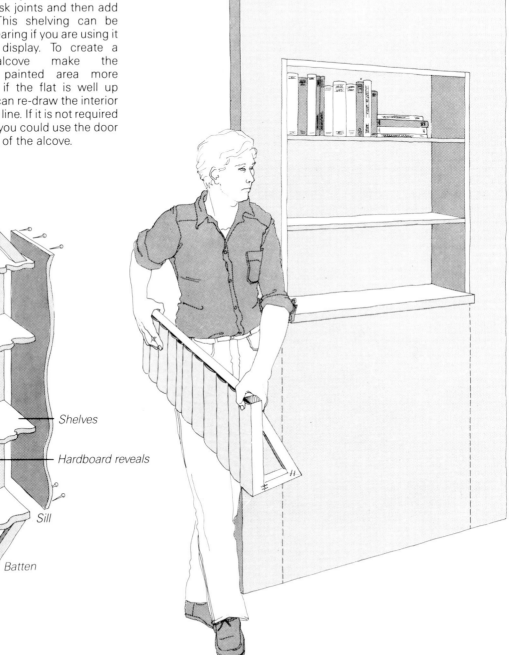

Shelves

Hardboard reveals

Sill

Batten

Ground rows and cut-outs

The term ground row is used to describe useful horizontal two-dimensional pieces of scenery built to create contour on the stage floor or at ground level. In addition this scenery can mask rostra, ramps and other acting levels, can create a variety of line and accentuate linear perspective. The ground row is a simple device requiring the minimum of support or bracing and is easily stored.

Making a ground row

First draw the outline on to hardboard or plywood. If you use an electric jigsaw draw on the reverse side, as the blade tends to pull upwards as it cuts and can splinter the edge. Do not make the ground row too heavy. Nail and glue timber battens to the base. Add vertical sections where the french braces are to be hinged. Make sure that the ground row is stable, and does not easily pull forward. Add temporary weights to the bottom of the brace to secure it in an upright position.

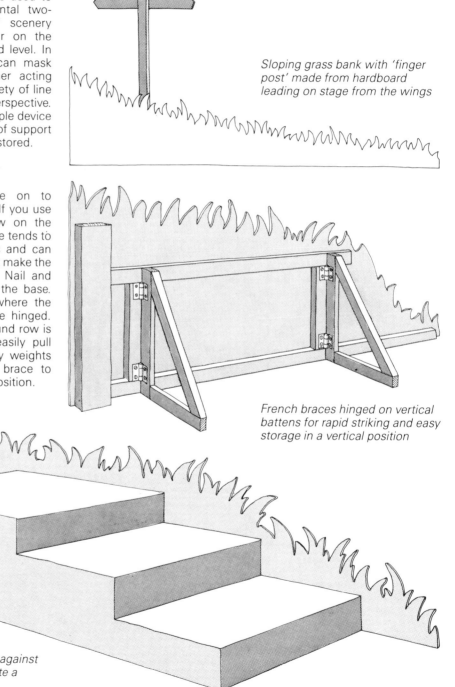

Sloping grass bank with 'finger post' made from hardboard leading on stage from the wings

French braces hinged on vertical battens for rapid striking and easy storage in a vertical position

A ground row mounted against steps and rostra to create a higher level entrance

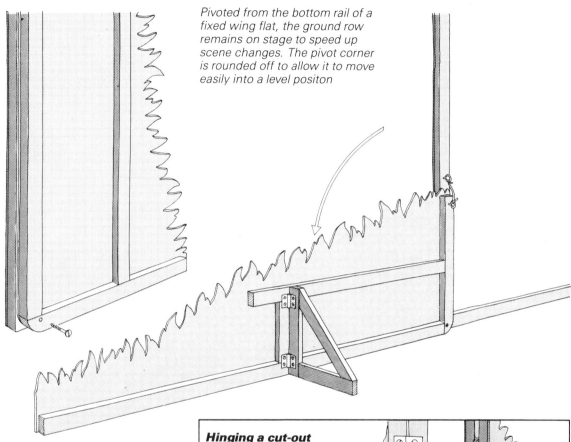

Pivoted from the bottom rail of a fixed wing flat, the ground row remains on stage to speed up scene changes. The pivot corner is rounded off to allow it to move easily into a level positon

When the ground row is in a level position the hinged french brace is pulled out

Where backstage space is short and time is important the designer can pivot or hinge ground rows on to existing flats. Position the ground row behind the wing flat. Screw the corner of the ground row into the bottom rail of the flat. (You may need to round off the ground row corner to ease movement.) If the row is long, screw a folding french brace at its mid-point. A simple hook and eye will secure the tape edge. Reinforce any part of the cut-out from behind.

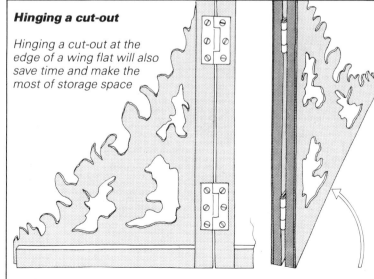

Hinging a cut-out

Hinging a cut-out at the edge of a wing flat will also save time and make the most of storage space

Ground rows and cut-outs

The profile of plain flats can be altered by the addition of hardboard to the leading edges. Perspective lines can also be reinforced with this extra scenery.

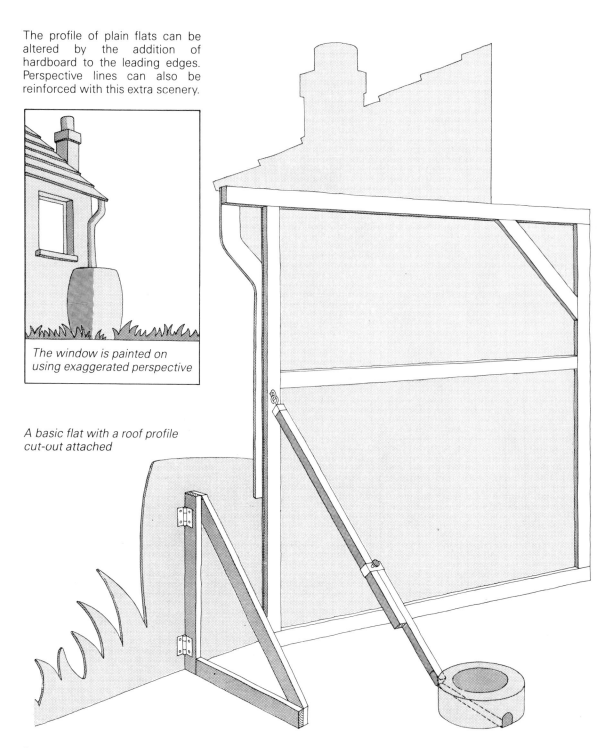

The window is painted on using exaggerated perspective

A basic flat with a roof profile cut-out attached

Trucked ground row

This device is ideal for simple settings of curtain and cyclorama. It must have an interesting shape and be cleverly lit, especially when it is the sole piece of scenery. The movement of its silhouette against a cyclorama or illuminated sky-cloth can be very attractive. Built as a tower structure it may also be illuminated from within, adding still more interest. Design the structure to allow entry.

A single trucked unit capable of setting the scene for four locations. All four faces compliment each other

Allow sufficient electric cable for changes of position

Paint the interior dark blue or black to reinforce the silhouette illusion. Cut out windows, doors, etc., and light from within

Rostra or platform blocks

On any stage, different acting levels provide variety and stimulation. They are an aid to visibility, particularly when the auditorium is level with, or below, the main acting surface. (Audiences become restive if they can only see the tops of the actors' heads!) When designing a set — aim high.

Rostra can be made so that they fold for easy storage or so that they remain as permanent constructions. They can be built in the form of boxes, ramps, curved sections, or a combination of these shapes. In every case however, you must make them strong. Remember they must bear considerable human traffic and need to be adequately reinforced to do so.

Folding rostra

By hinging the leg units in the manner illustrated you can make accurate right angled corners. The top cover cross battens may then be cut to ensure a snug fit when laid over the leg construction. By using a nail as a replacement of the hinge pin, storage is made even more simple (see page 60).

The sides of the rostra are constructed by fixing an upper and lower rail into the corner stile. Use mortise and tenon joints for maximum strength. The rails make the rostra as light as possible and easy to move about the stage.

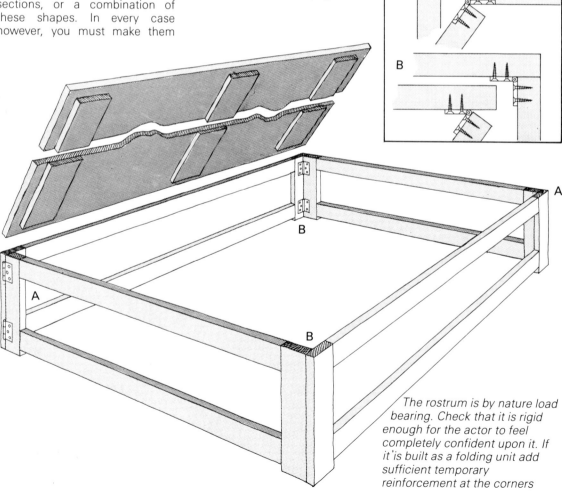

The rostrum is by nature load bearing. Check that it is rigid enough for the actor to feel completely confident upon it. If it is built as a folding unit add sufficient temporary reinforcement at the corners

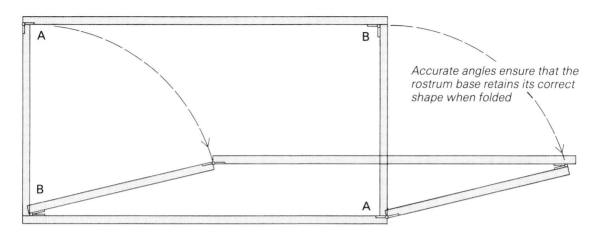

Accurate angles ensure that the rostrum base retains its correct shape when folded

Ramps

Although this scenery occupies more stage space, actors may move with more confidence from one level to another rather than using steps.

If the ramp width exceeds 3 feet (90cm), a central support is advised. Do not make the slope unnecessarily severe.

These structures are not foldable, but can on occasions be used as sloping wall units — as in a castle wall or, properly weighted at the base, as free standing set units such as buttresses.

Where the top edge of the ramp base and the surface meet it may be necessary to glue strips of sponge or rubber to prevent friction or squeaking

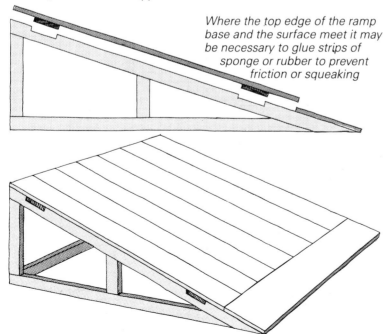

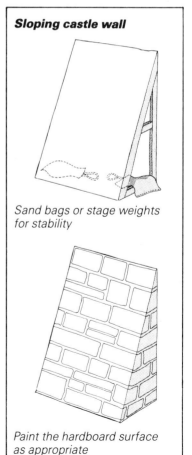

Sloping castle wall

Sand bags or stage weights for stability

Paint the hardboard surface as appropriate

Rostra or platform blocks

Trucks or wagons

Very simply the truck is a platform mounted on swivel casters which can be moved about the stage with ease. Dimensions can vary to suit the task — it can carry a complete setting or just one small part of it (see page 80).

For stage setting purposes the minimum dimensions should be 4 feet x 6 feet 6 inches (121 x 198 cm) and not exceed 8 inches (20 cm) above stage level.

Casters are very important and should be as large as possible. A 3½ inch (90 mm) rubber tired swivel caster is ideal. It must turn through 360° and have a ball bearing seating and a sturdy bed plate for efficient movement.

The platform itself must be sturdily constructed and, within reason, be as heavy as possible to provide a secure base for flats and other tall scenery. The clearance between truck and stage level is important and should not exceed 1 inch (25 mm).

Take trouble over joints; glue and screw, and if necessary reinforce angles with braces or blocks.

Screw the caster plate firmly at the ends of planks 4 feet long by 6 inches wide (121 x 15cm) and at least 1 inch (25 mm) thick. Position the plate so that the caster can rotate freely through the 360° without contacting the timber skirt of the truck.

Cut the side skirt planks as illustrated. The depth of join is dictated by the thickness of the caster-bearing planks.

Glue and screw the caster planks on to the skirt planking. Check that they are level and that the casters are set below the bottom edge.

In the illustration a housing joint is shown at the center of the side skirt planking. This will house a support batten along the truck length to give added stability and avoid sag or bounce. An additional set of casters can be screwed to this to give increased stability and ease of movement. Lay the surface of blockboard or plywood over the structure. This should measure 6 feet (182 cm) plus the thickness of the two end sections of the skirt to enable you to screw the surface down into each edge of the skirting timber. This is necessary because the long skirt planks are end grained and so not reliable when nailing or screwing. Use extra long nails or screws to secure and glue.

To prevent movement when loaded, tether wooden wedges at either end. Shape a pocket into which each wedge may be stored when the truck is moved. The nature of the truck may mean that support blocks are nailed on to it to help stabilize the flats.

Scenery built upon the truck must be self supporting and rigid. It will be necessary to nail and screw into the timberwork bases of flats and secure the tops and sides. (See page 80.)

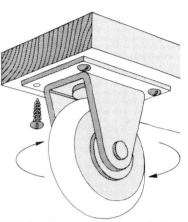

1 *Use large casters with 360° swivel and ball race seating*

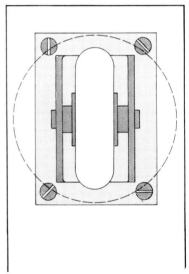

2 *Screw the caster plates at each end of the plank. Ensure that they can rotate freely*

3 *Cut away from the side skirt planks to the depth of the caster-bearing planks*

6 ft 6 ins (198 cm)

7 ins (18cm)

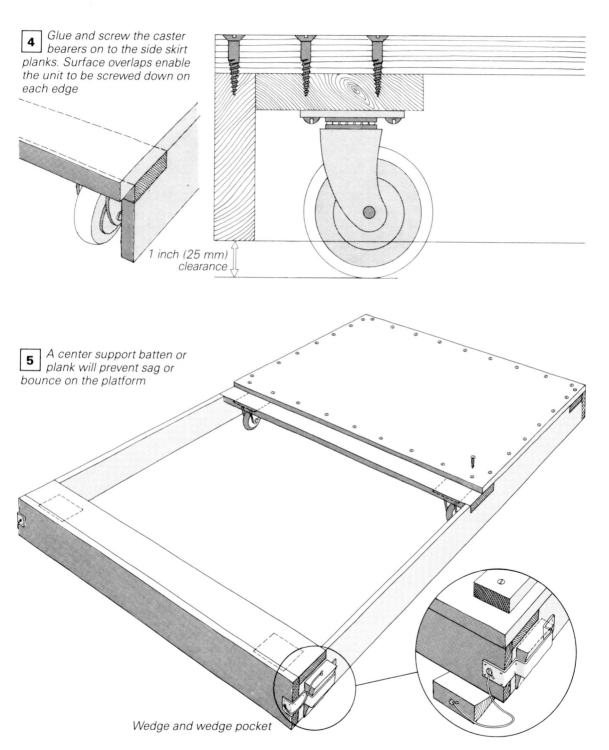

4 Glue and screw the caster bearers on to the side skirt planks. Surface overlaps enable the unit to be screwed down on each edge

1 inch (25 mm) clearance

5 A center support batten or plank will prevent sag or bounce on the platform

Wedge and wedge pocket

Devices for saving time and space

Double-sided flats

The drawing of scene end tabs and the time taken to change the set can break the spell woven by the preceding act. Aim for as smooth, speedy and effective a change as possible. A shortage of space and manpower often means developing novel ways of quickening the scene changes and in certain productions the changes themselves have proved more effective when made in full view of the audience.

A useful time-saver when changing sets is to build into the design two or three standard flats covered with canvas on both sides. (Hardboard is heavy and places undue strain on the host flat.) Reversing or folding back this double-sided flat will radically alter the scene.

Before covering the back of the flat, remove the cleats, throw line and any other flat furniture. Fit on a split hinge section some 2 feet (60 cm) from each end. Screw the hinge mate on to the host flat remembering to allow a half-inch (12 mm) floor clearance to swing the flat over the stage. If the flat is wider than 3 feet (90 cm) it is worth attaching a small caster to the outer stile of the hinged flat. Glue and tack canvas or sack cloth to the back of the flat to cover the hinge seating. When the flats have been hinged together glue on a strip of canvas to help disguise the unavoidable gap between the two flats.

By repeating this arrangement on both sides of the set an interior setting can be changed to an exterior setting in seconds. The scheme can also be adapted to include three or four flats of differing widths and functions.

Add extra bracing to the host flats and a string or hook to the outside edge of the swinging flat to prevent swaying. The foot of the flat can be held in position by a tight wedge.

Lighter, smaller flats can be attached by canvas hinges as an alternative to metal hinges and these have the advantage of folding back both ways.

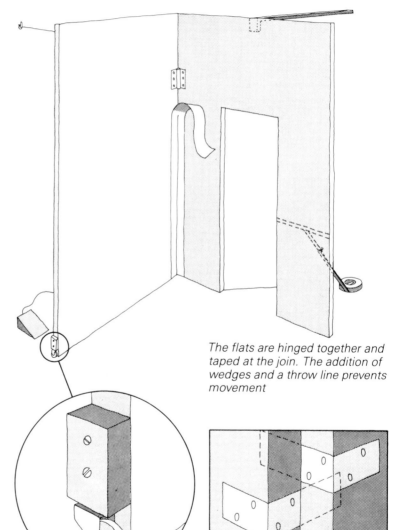

The flats are hinged together and taped at the join. The addition of wedges and a throw line prevents movement

A caster on the outside of the hinged flat provides support and smooth mobility

A two-way canvas hinge can also be used to connect two lightweight flats together

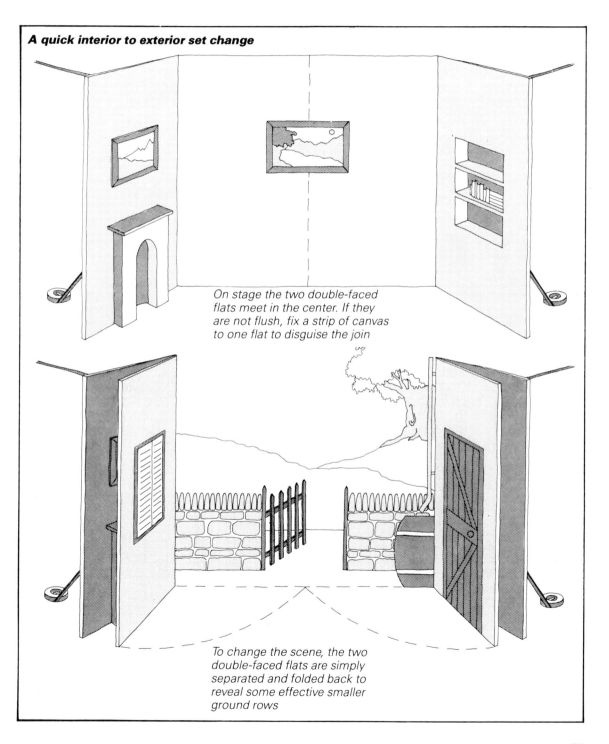

A quick interior to exterior set change

On stage the two double-faced flats meet in the center. If they are not flush, fix a strip of canvas to one flat to disguise the join

To change the scene, the two double-faced flats are simply separated and folded back to reveal some effective smaller ground rows

Devices for saving time and space

Horizontal overlapping leaves

This technique for quick change scenery is similar to double-sided flats except that the hinge is horizontal rather than vertical. You will need to convert a standard flat or door flat, depending on the size of the leaf required. The host flat is set with the timber construction facing towards the audience or down stage. The overlap leaf is painted on both sides and is hinged to the lower toggle rail. This arrangement is usually most effective from the front elevation. It can be used on the side walls but it will require an architrave or timber batten to mask the edge join which may not be consistent with the lines of the general set design.

You may experience difficulty screwing hinges to thin hardboard. The alternative is to make canvas hinges or to nail a thin strip of timber on to the hardboard which will provide a more secure base for the hinge. A small bolt or twin latches are sufficient to hold the leaf in position. These can be positioned on the up stage side or masked and painted over.

If more detail is required, the thickness of the props used is critical to any deception. Shelves filled with glued on paper plates or book spines look authentic. Make 'body' by cutting kitchen roll tubes in half, placing them side by side and gluing them to a piece of cardboard. A shadowed background creates an extra illusion of depth. (See page 124).

The eye is easily distracted by a reflecting surface, so avoid shiny objects and take care that props do not hinder the overlapping leaf when it is folded over.

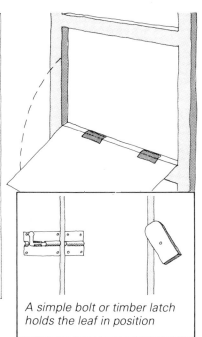

Reversed flat which will have an overlapping leaf hinged on its lower toggle rail

A simple bolt or timber latch holds the leaf in position

The illusion of depth is easily added by shading and highlighting with a paint brush

The center leaf folds down to cover the fireplace and display a bookshelf and wall decoration

Three-dimensional leaves

A lightweight box construction can be used most effectively with a door flat as a host. The box 'leaf' measurements must allow sufficient leeway for the unit to fit within the doorway. Although somewhat more weighty than the single thickness leaf, the mechanics remain the same and the set change becomes even more dramatic.

Insert a rail between the door frame to carry the hinges. Measure the space to allow for the width of the box leaf and add a masking piece to cover any remaining gap. The leaf is secured with a small bolt or twin latch as illustrated.

Cover the remainder of the door flat construction with hardboard. Check that the established method of bracing the host flat is sufficient to bear the movement of weightier box leaves.

Once the general principles have been mastered, variations on this theme can be developed and small problems of detail solved.

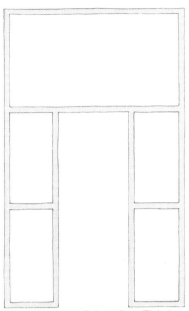

Reverse view of door flat. This is used to contain the heavier construction of a box leaf

Shelved unit screwed to toggle rail measures the same as the inside doorway

Paper plates and book spines

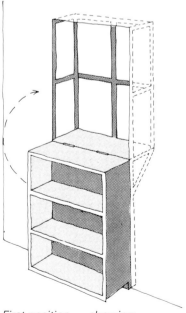

First position — showing bookshelf and window

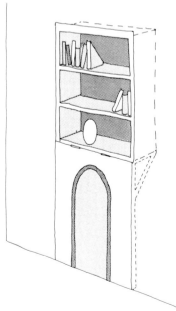

Second position — revealing a fireplace

Devices for saving time and space

Multi-purpose units

Some multi-purpose units are complicated constructions with many joints and hinges. Their construction may require a high degree of technical expertise. Building them will absorb much of the time of your most skilled woodworker and you must decide whether this is the most efficient use of time and effort.

If you do go ahead, first make clear working drawings and a small model to demonstrate the operating method.

The simplest unit is the reversible flat. This is particularly suitable for curtained sets or for stages with low ceilings. Set a socket into the stage floor and a short spindle into the center bottom rail of a double-sided flat. Fit a matching spindle from the top rail into a socket in the ceiling grid. This will turn easily and can be held in position by a wedge. Paint in contrasting colors to accentuate the change.

Arch sections, hinged on a flat, can simply be folded back for one setting and brought forward for the change. A central keystone attached to one flat will be sufficient to hide the join.

Quick change token scenery is well suited to the fast pace of farce and pantomime but the success

depends on the effective disguise of the second or third face of the unit so that the audience's attention is not diverted.

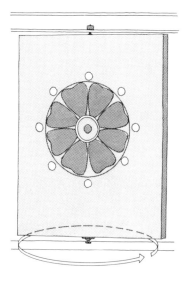

Double-sided wing flat showing the two short spindles inserted into floor and ceiling sockets

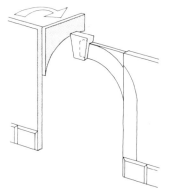

Arch sections hinged to hold flats. A central keystone hides the join and can be a feature

---

A host truck

A platform no larger than 3 x 2 feet (90 x 60 cm) can be maneuvered easily and set in position with the minimum of fuss. Mortises cut into the surface take the legs of the passenger unit. Desks, pulpits, pumps, cabinets and other awkwardly shaped pieces can then be wheeled on and off stage with ease

A combination of trucking and flying can work well. First build a pillar from cardboard and an old tire and mount it on a small truck. Use this in conjunction with a flown arch. The position of the truck should be marked clearly on the stage floor with masking tape or chalk and the arch lowered on top. Make sure you place wedges under the truck once it is in its correct place on stage.

Careful painting will add all the necessary illusion. Larger trucks with double-sided flats and vertical and horizontal hinges offer a greater scale of change than the smaller truck but correspondingly greater versatility. Box units, with casters can also present a variety of faces.

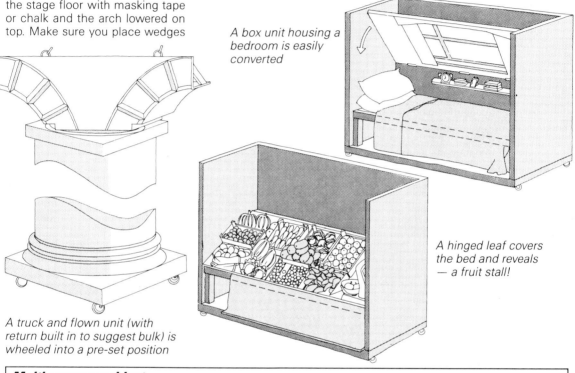

A box unit housing a bedroom is easily converted

A hinged leaf covers the bed and reveals — a fruit stall!

A truck and flown unit (with return built in to suggest bulk) is wheeled into a pre-set position

Multi-purpose cabinet

A box unit is easily transferred from bar to display shelves before conversion to a blackboard and easel

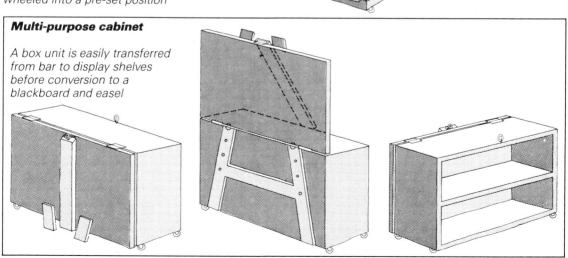

Devices for saving time and space

Trucks and wagons

No theater group should be without at least one well made truck (see page 72). Time and again it will answer your staging and storage problems and prove an indispensible and adaptable workhorse.

The truck will roll easily about the stage carrying considerable weight, and will remove dependence on traditional scene changing techniques.

The most versatile of flat arrangements on a truck is a three-sided arrangement. When the 'open' side is out of sight it can be refurnished or re-set. Merely a change of drape or furniture is often all that is required. If you are saddled with a wide but shallow stage, the truck may be moved in parallel to the setting or traverse curtain line from side to side. A narrow but deep stage will enable you to rotate the truck through 360° and vary the possibilities still more. Construction of two trucks will more than double the options open to you.

Do not feel that you must disguise the movement of this truck system. If the movement is made smoothly in full view of the audience it will please and sometimes mystify them. It avoids interruption caused by drawing front tabs. Today's theater audience is familiar with scene changes on stage.

The professional theater and amateur groups differ in their attitude to scenery. The professionals, whilst salvaging as much as possible from previous productions, also discard quite freely. The amateur, however, has a tendency to hoard useless and bulky stock. The amateur also tends to construct even the most simple flat in the traditional manner, whereas time and cost saving methods are essential to the professional. Heavy duty staples are often used to secure canvas to frames rather than tacks, and the simple butt joint is often employed. The rail is fixed to the stile with corrugated fasteners and reinforced by a triangular plywood plate that is glued and screwed over the corner.

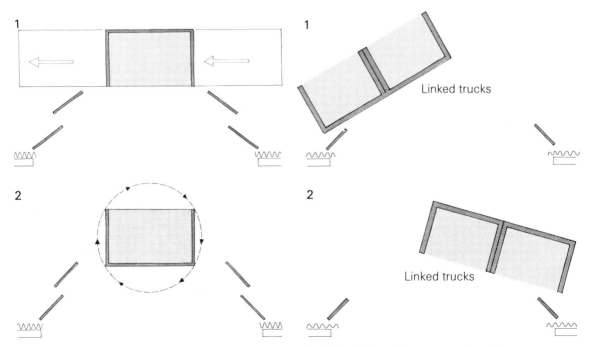

Position 1 Open face of truck towards audience
Position 2 Closed face towards audience

Position 1 Closed face towards audience
Position 2 Open face towards audience

Temporary fastenings and joints

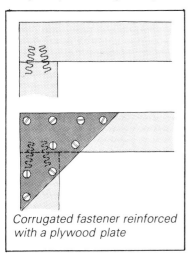

Corrugated fastener reinforced with a plywood plate

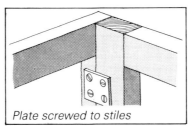

Plate screwed to stiles

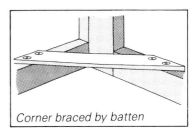

Corner braced by batten

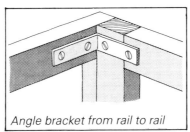

Angle bracket from rail to rail

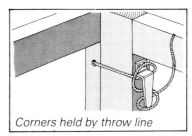

Corners held by throw line

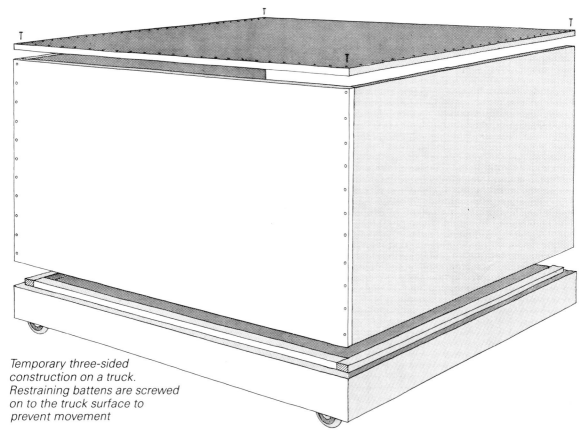

Temporary three-sided construction on a truck. Restraining battens are screwed on to the truck surface to prevent movement

Cyclorama

A cyclorama is an area of canvas placed at the furthest position up stage away from the audience. Though movable it is usually permanently positioned with sufficient room between it and the rear wall to allow cross stage movement. The canvas is sometimes stretched between curved frames to give the impression of sky, hence its other name, 'sky-cloth'. Because of the smooth, taut surface of the stretched canvas the cyclorama is an ideal lighting background.

The designer can create a sense of greater space and atmosphere with a well-lit cyclorama. There is no need for a pulley set. Curtains and rostra and props with a strong silhouette combine with the lighting effects to show the changing pattern of the real sky.

How to build a cyclorama

Ideally the cloth should be supported within a curved structure but small stages rarely have the space to make this worth while. Stitch tapes on to, or eyelets into, a piece of canvas large enough to cover the back wall of the stage. These tapes should be tightened as the canvas stretches over a period of time.

1

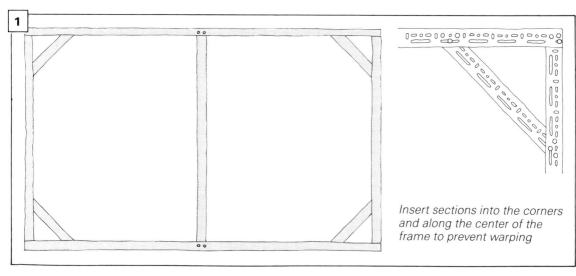

Insert sections into the corners and along the center of the frame to prevent warping

2

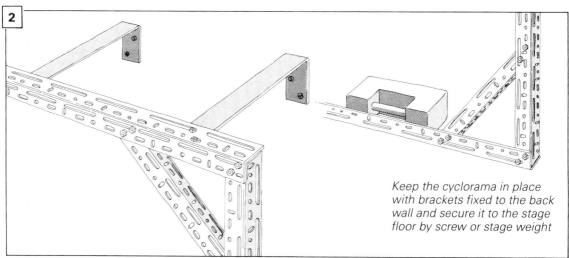

Keep the cyclorama in place with brackets fixed to the back wall and secure it to the stage floor by screw or stage weight

3

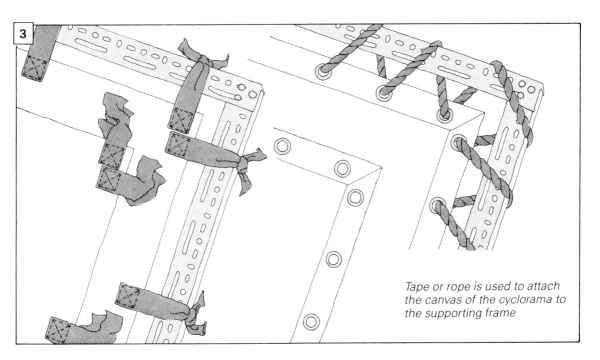

Tape or rope is used to attach the canvas of the cyclorama to the supporting frame

Place the tapes or eyelets about 1 foot (30 cm) apart. Bolt together slotted angle frame sections. Reinforce the frame at the center and at each corner to prevent warping.

Position the frame at least 3 feet (90 cm) from the back wall and secure it to the wall and to the stage floor.

Tie or rope the canvas to the top rail so that it hangs straight down. Allow it to hang for a while so that its weight will pull out any creases.

Tape or rope down the canvas at each side of the frame simultaneously, not too firmly, and finally secure the bottom edge.

Do not fix the lashings too tightly, as when you have sized the surface the canvas will shrink. Make any necessary adjustments to maintain an even surface.

Back wall

Brace | Cyclorama | 3ft (90 cm) | Brace

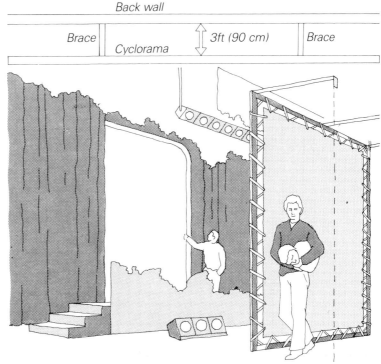

Cyclorama

Lighting the cyclorama

All lighting must be positioned at least 3 feet (90 cm) away from the cloth to avoid a patchy effect. It should also be angled so that the light diffuses over the canvas. If the lights are at stage level it will probably be necessary to mask them with a rostrum or ground row. Side lighting can be hidden by the wing curtains or flats and top lighting disguised with borders hung from the ceiling.

It is perhaps these prerequisites which restrict the installation of cycloramas on stages lacking in depth. However the design benefits far outweigh the disadvantages. If you cannot afford the space to erect a cyclorama, make use of the back stage wall. Plaster or fill the wall to achieve a smooth finish and paint it white. It may restrict backstage movement but the final effect is worth the inconvenience.

Scenery used in conjunction with the cyclorama should be designed primarily for a two-dimensional effect and should be in keeping with the simple design concept, uncomplicated and not fussy.

Mask both the top and sides of standard flats to prevent the strong light from the cyclorama shining through gaps.

Slender pillars, arches, irregular roof-lines, all have more impact when lit from behind. Furniture used in these settings should be in the form of simple shapes. If necessary add profiles in hardboard or plywood to change their silhouette.

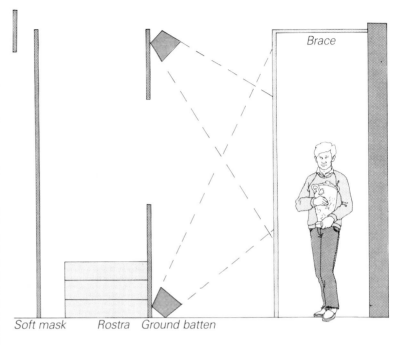

Soft mask   Rostra   Ground batten

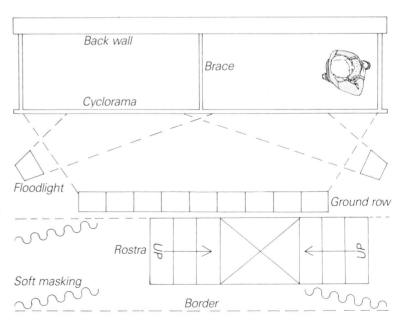

Back wall

Brace

Cyclorama

Floodlight

Ground row

Rostra   UP   UP

Soft masking

Border

Side elevation and plan for lighting the cyclorama

Use of curtains with cyclorama

Experiment with different curtain settings, pulling only one side of a traverse to partially reveal the cyclorama, or perhaps widening or narrowing the view of the cyclorama. By lowering a border or by the positioning of ground rows the cyclorama can also be 'squeezed'. The designer may change a scene with very little effort or delay.

When used in conjunction with a cyclorama, curtains become more prominent and contribute more to the setting. Boldly patterned material is an improvement on single color leg curtains and can add a color richness which will compliment the simplicity of the design without dominating the stage too much.

A cyclorama or sky-cloth can be used outside the proscenium arched stage. If it is planned to use it in an arena setting however, a curtain structure must be made to frame the unit properly.

A simple setting for a journey, using a half curtain, stage right, with a tree profile and finger post

A narrower gap displays an effective flown stained glass window with an altar and candelabra in profile

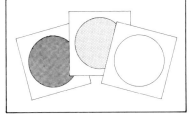

Partly-closed traverse curtains reveal a throne, flown crown, and interesting property silhouettes

Stage ceiling and fly space

The changing tastes of the theater going public have encouraged a less conventional approach to the presentation of plays. Stock scenery is no longer considered essential. Materials such as timber and canvas have risen sharply in price and many items of ironmongery are now difficult to obtain. However, there remains a need to disguise or mask backstage activity. This is best achieved with a simple curtain set, front wing or leg curtains and a traverse cloth. Other soft scenic devices like back-cloths, gauzes and cut cloths are often sufficient to create the right dramatic effect. All these need a superstructure from which they may be hung.

In older buildings with pitched roofs, joists and beams are, of necessity, sturdy enough to bear the weight of the roof tiles. Modern roofing methods rely on less heavy materials supported by strategically placed steel joists.

If your venue has an existing stage but no proscenium, a super structure will require strong support. (The weight of curtain material alone is considerable.) If your landlord aproves and your tenure is secure this support structure could remain as a permanent unit.

You will require considerable lengths of slotted steel angle or scaffolding poles which should be bolted or welded together. The feet of this structure need to be screwed or bolted into the floor or stage surface to prevent any creeping when the structure is under stress. It should be as high as possible but allow space for the stage furniture to work unhindered. Reinforce all the corners, and if the horizontal lengths are too long you may need

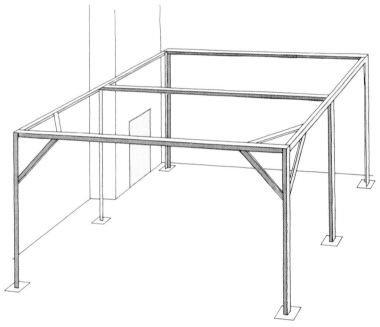

Slotted steel angle or scaffolding poles are bolted or welded together to form a support structure. Floor plates screwed to the stage add stability

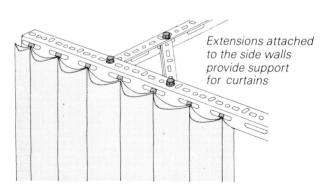

Extensions attached to the side walls provide support for curtains

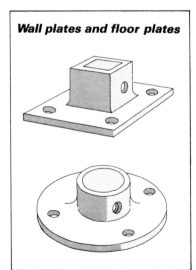

Wall plates and floor plates

to supply intermediate support. Try, if possible, to position these extra fixtures across the width rather than fore and aft. This will facilitate lifting and flying.

Having built the skeleton it is a comparatively simple task to add the necessary curtain support units. Bolt on sections of lighter weight angle of sufficient length to reach the side walls.

The task is much simpler if your stage has an existing proscenium arch. Check that the proscenium wall is load bearing. Frequently it is merely lightly covered with little intrinsic strength. You may need to reinforce its vertical strength with metal or timber. If the back wall of the stage area is load bearing the task is simplified still further. Bolt a plate on to the back wall and affix the horizontal bearer on to it.

A pitched roof will enable you to extend this basic support structure. Build upon the main structure a further scaffold 'box' to maximize the space available. This extra height will enable you to fly items — albeit of limited dimensions.

Those stages with a load bearing ceiling of steel joists or substantial beams may be used to suspend lightweight superstructure, but the combined weight of stage ceiling furniture and lighting is very considerable and unless you are advised professionally as to the load bearing capacity of those roof joists you should consider the leg supports illustrated. Use steel cable rather than rope if the anchorage is secure and you own heavy duty winches. The cabling can be arranged to allow lowering of the superstructure but secure mounting is to be recommended for this critical structure.

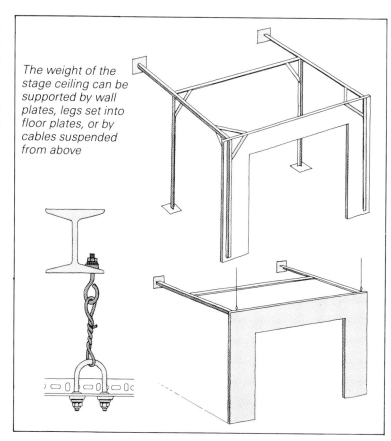

The weight of the stage ceiling can be supported by wall plates, legs set into floor plates, or by cables suspended from above

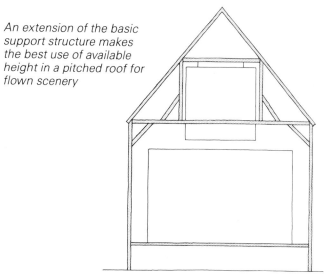

An extension of the basic support structure makes the best use of available height in a pitched roof for flown scenery

Stage ceiling and fly space

Stage ceiling grid

Stages which boast load bearing walls to front and rear need only install fore and aft members to form a superstructure from which the ceiling grid may then be suspended.

The grid is easily constructed from 2 inch (50 mm) tubular welded alloy slotted angle, box section steel. Intermediate members should be laid across the width of the stage. Fore/aft members may obstruct lifting.

The grid dimensions should match the general operating stage area but allow space up stage to alter the cyclorama position and down stage at the proscenium to allow unhindered operation of the front tabs. This grid will bear the weight of curtains, traverse battens and lighting units. It can be wired to allow lifting and lowering of the grid for periodic maintenance.

Once you have the basic superstructure and grid firmly in place you can add tracks, traverses and battens to hold the ceiling furniture. The rigidity and stability of these cross battens will depend on the width of the stage. You may need to compensate for sagging with additional stiffening.

The border curtain battens will require frequent adjustment to enable them to curtail and control vertical sight-lines.

On low stages borders attached to piping, lying above the grid, may simply be pushed with a long pole, but for larger, higher stages a more secure bracket or bolt should be attached.

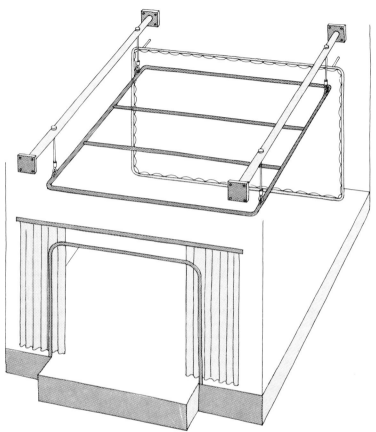

The ceiling grid is suspended from the superstructure by cable

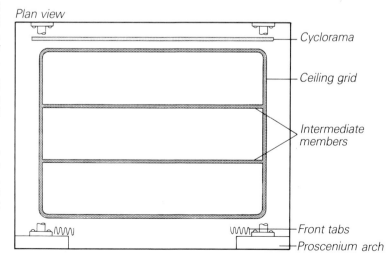

Plan view

— Cyclorama

— Ceiling grid

— Intermediate members

— Front tabs

— Proscenium arch

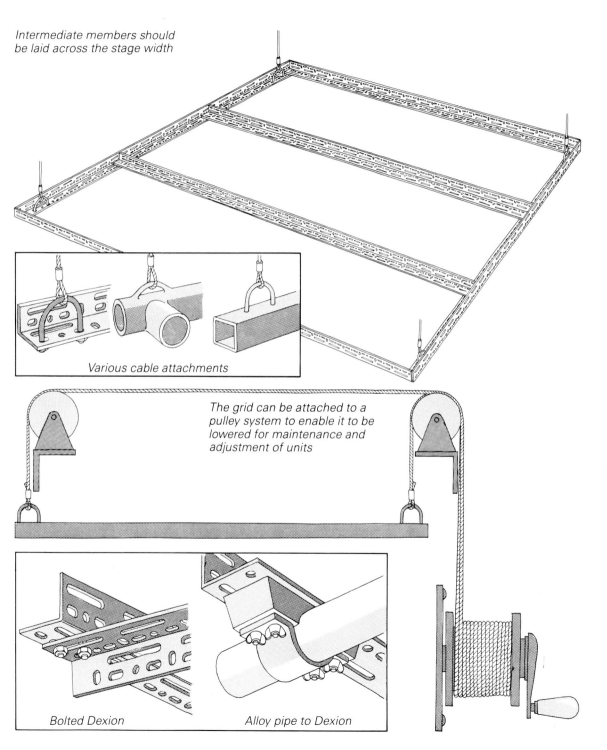

*Intermediate members should
be laid across the stage width*

Various cable attachments

*The grid can be attached to a
pulley system to enable it to be
lowered for maintenance and
adjustment of units*

Bolted Dexion

Alloy pipe to Dexion

Stage ceiling furniture

The stage ceiling

Stage ceiling space is always valuable. Whereas flats, rostra and other stage-mounted scenery are mostly interconnected, the ceiling holds a mass of ropes, pulleys, battens as well as lighting units. Space is therefore at a premium and should be sensibly allocated. As most stage lighting is positioned behind the proscenium to make it work effectively, planning the ceiling arrangement needs considerable thought and organization.

The following pages deal with this aspect of scene distribution and design. Try to vary the schemes suggested to suit your backstage area, stage height and strength. Make the most of it. Once a basic curtain set has been tried and tested, the progression toward other types of presentation may be made more confidently.

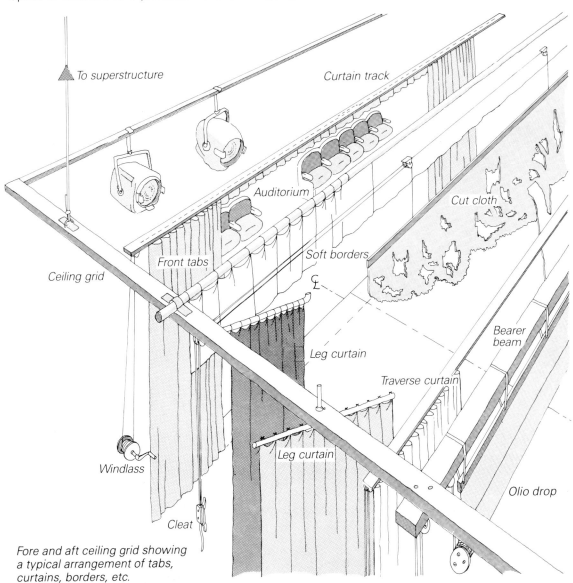

To superstructure

Curtain track

Auditorium

Cut cloth

Ceiling grid

Front tabs

Soft borders

℄

Leg curtain

Bearer beam

Traverse curtain

Windlass

Leg curtain

Olio drop

Cleat

Fore and aft ceiling grid showing a typical arrangement of tabs, curtains, borders, etc.

Scenery hardware

The essential mobility of scenery has led to the design of hardware to brace, stiffen, join and lift components. Although some items are readily available, the more specialized may need to be obtained from appropriate manufacturers.

Here are some suggestions for bolts and hooks which may prove useful to you.

Hanger iron straight and hooked

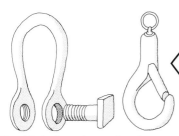

Shackle bolt and snap hook

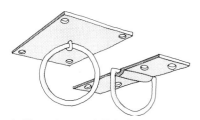

Ceiling plate and 'D' plate

Turnbuckle

Ropes and cables

It is often tempting to buy the cheapest available for rigging purposes, but the 'fibrous' nylon ropes are both hard on the hand and prone to tangle. Sash cord is ideal for lightweight rigging but generally cotton braid and stranded manila are preferable. Wire or cable is necessary to suspend stationary units such as the ceiling grid and the load-bearing pulleys. It is strong in relation to its diameter and may be used to suspend items of scenery where the cable is visible.

Pulleys and cleats

These vary in size and application. A variety is required if there is a level of tripping involved (see page 97). Single and multiple pulleys and sheaves are available in both hanging and plated form.

Make certain that pulleys and cleats are well founded. Many will carry considerable weight and will be sited in a potentially dangerous position overhead. It is a good idea to mount the plated pulleys on blockboard first, if the surface is unsuitable or if there is any doubt about their security.

The pulleys bearing most weight should be secured by cable to the ceiling grid or superstructure. Try where possible to set up a continuous loop of rope. This will avoid unwieldy lengths of rope trailing on the stage floor. While the stage crew are aware of the hazards of stage clutter, the cast are frequently preoccupied with their lines or have their eyes on the stars seeking inspiration.

All ropes and cables, unless winched, must be tied off on cleats. These can be single or

double and can easily be made from wood to suit their particular purpose. Again, it is vital to ensure that the board or plank bearing the cleats is screwed securely to the stage wall.

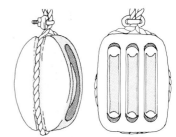

Wooden sheave with cable

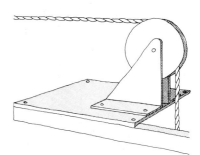

Heavy duty pulley with bed plate mounted on blockboard

The correct way to tie off a rope on single and double cleats

Stage ceiling furniture

Traverse or traveler curtain tracking

The proscenium tabs are the most obvious examples of traverse curtains. Swiftly drawn they can create an impressive dramatic movement. There are numerous designs of track — all of which are well tried and efficient. To achieve the desired effect and to be relatively sound proof, the curtains need to be lined as well as weighted in the bottom hem. This increases the overall weight and requires a commensurate strength in the track design.

A continuous rope or cord arrangement is recommended for smoothness of action. This will enable the stage manager to operate the pulley and draw the curtain without moving from his position in the wings. This is a system more appropriate for the upstage traverse curtains. The curtains are less heavy and the demand on the track is therefore reduced. Speed of drawing is not as important in this scene setting position.

A windlass (illustrated below) is both smooth and swift and is a good investment.

The tracks themselves require careful and regular lubrication to prevent any metallic sound intruding upon the soft 'swish' of the curtain material. Four different types of commercially made tracks are illustrated below.

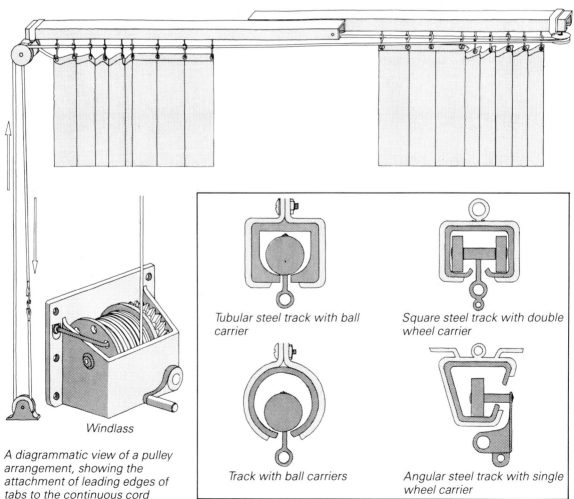

Windlass

A diagrammatic view of a pulley arrangement, showing the attachment of leading edges of tabs to the continuous cord

Tubular steel track with ball carrier

Square steel track with double wheel carrier

Track with ball carriers

Angular steel track with single wheel carrier

Simple swivel bolt and batten

Drill a hole through the fore and aft member and insert a bolt. Fix the wing curtain to a wooden section as shown and drill a hole in the center. Insert the bolt through the wing batten and through the main support member and screw on a wing nut to make it secure. Some lead shot inserted into the bottom hem will provide weight.

Adjustable swivel

If, to avoid making holes in the wing curtains you decide to attach tie tapes, or if you need different length curtains to fit in with a rostra assembly, this may prove a more flexible system.

Weld two pieces of rod into a T shape as shown.

Drill a hole into the fore and aft grid member if it is timber or alloy tube. Tie on the leg curtains.

A metal collar with securing nut will enable you to vary the T frame height as necessary.

Sleeve attachment

If you have a particularly low ceiling, screw a tubular metal 'sleeve' to the main member. Bend the end of a section of pipe to fit into the sleeve and attach the leg curtains to the pipe either by curtain rings or with tie tapes. You can vary the angle considerably with this method.

Change the mood simply by fixing different color wing curtains on either side of the batten, and reversing its position.

A bolt secured with a wing nut is screwed through the fore and aft member of the ceiling grid through the wing curtain batten

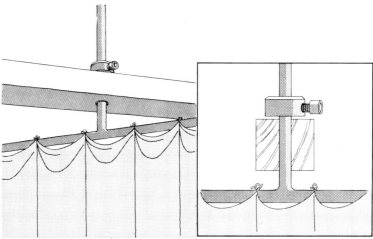

Leg curtains are easily adjusted by using this swivel method

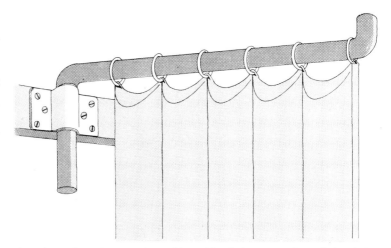

A variety of angles can be achieved by fitting a section of pipe into a sleeve on the main support

Stage ceiling furniture

Curtains

Border, leg, or wing and traverse curtains create the simplest of all stage settings. In neutral colors they provide an excellent background where only light and costume are required to underline the mood and setting. This 'soft masking' depends upon uncomplicated supports structures to be efficient.

Border battens

These support the border curtains which are important in masking the often cluttered fly area. They are useful in both curtain and box settings. In box settings an alternative is a 'hard mask'; a flat or lightly constructed unit is suspended horizontally above the stage, producing a level ceiling to the set suitable for painting. This is best suspended by the normal pulley system and if necessary can be set at an angle with bridled rope work.

Curtains however are lighter and more versatile. They may be hung from simple alloy piping, slotted angle or timber battens, and can be positioned under or over the ceiling grid. A lightweight clip and wing nut is sufficient to hold the curtain in position below the grid but if you choose to lay it above the grid ensure that you allow sufficient length to overlap. On small stages adjustments may be made simply by sliding the batten into position.

If the batten needs to bear more weight it must be firmly bolted. Lighting battens require extra bracing or support from the ceiling grid and unless bolted into position traverse curtain tracks will not be stable when drawn.

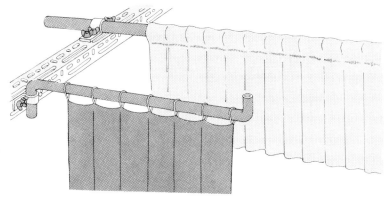

Borders and leg curtains attached to sleeved pipes are easily adjusted

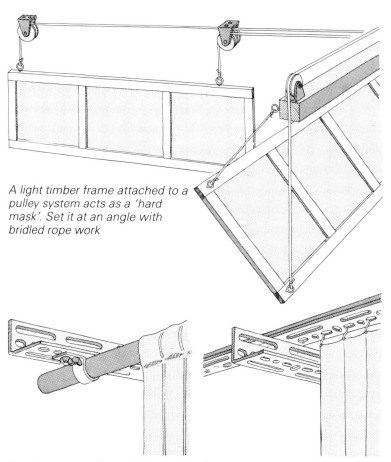

A light timber frame attached to a pulley system acts as a 'hard mask'. Set it at an angle with bridled rope work

Border support clipped and bolted under the ceiling grid

Support resting on top of the ceiling grid

The short borders must be attached to the batten so that the bottom edge is level and regularly pleated. They may be hooked, taped or sandwiched on to the batten. There is no need to add weight, lead shot or wire to the bottom hem. The material will 'fall' into place.

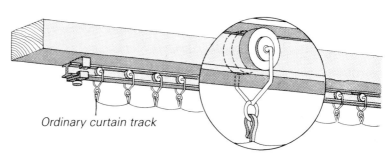

Ordinary curtain track

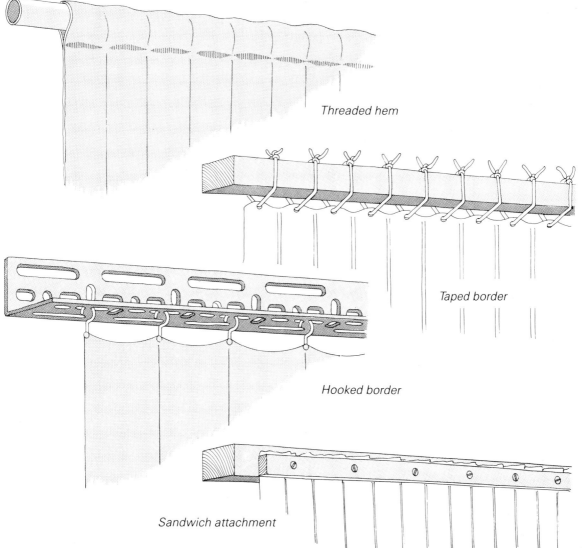

Threaded hem

Taped border

Hooked border

Sandwich attachment

Tripping scenery

Tripping is a system of folding a cloth or drop out of sight of the audience.

In all tripping work the pulley arrangement is the same. A single pulley is placed at one end and double pulleys used at the winching or operating side.

Rope work for rollers

If the bearer batten is bolted above the fore and aft ceiling grid member, position the single pulley above a hole drilled to allow rope through on the far side. Position the double pulley above a similar hole. Place the last double pulley in line with the others and drill two holes to allow easy passage of the ropes leading to the final securing cleat.

If the bearer batten is below the ceiling grid, screw the pulleys into position in the same alignment. Rope up and knot the rope tail into the roller. Take sufficient turns around the roller to ensure that the lead rope faces up stage i.e. clockwise on the left hand side and counterclockwise on the right. To raise the roller pull both ropes together. They will unwind as the roller lifts.

An alternative roping system for lifting the roller involves screwing an eye bolt into the .underside of the bearer batten to either side. The pulleys are then threaded as normal. Take one turn around the roller and then knot the rope on to the eye bolt. Using this system there is only one turn of rope around the roller at any one time. Lift the roller by pulling on both ropes as above. Encourage all stage hands to tie off ropes in the same way so that no one is struggling at a crucial moment.

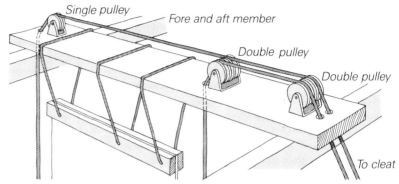

A standard pulley arrangement for all tripping systems

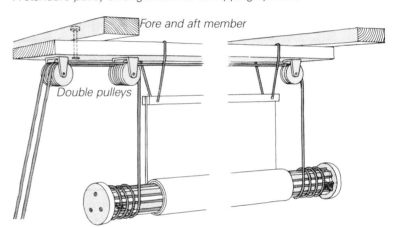

The rope is slotted into the roller so that the lead faces up stage
The roller is then raised by pulling on both ropes

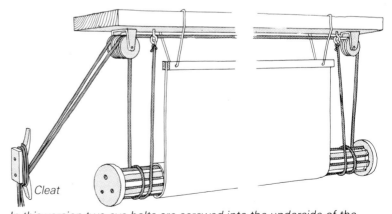

In this version two eye bolts are screwed into the underside of the bearer batten. The ropes are knotted to the eye bolts, passed around the roller once and then threaded through the pulley system. Pull on the ropes to raise the roller

Tripping light cloth

This roping system is suitable for soft pieces, although, if your ceiling space allows, it can also be applied to some limited light-weight pieces.

The top mechanism and arrangement of pulleys is the same as described for the olio roller on page 98. By inserting thin battens or rods into the cloth at chosen points you will also be able to vary the lifting positions. The maximum single lift will once again depend upon your ceiling or loft space. A combination of hard pieces and soft pieces can be lifted together. The hard piece needs to hang below the soft piece and it is important to keep it as light as possible. A large sheet of hardboard reinforced with thin batten is a rigid and fairly light construction. A simple housefront is a good example of this system. The soft piece forms the roof and the hardboard 'wall' is easily cut to make windows and doors.

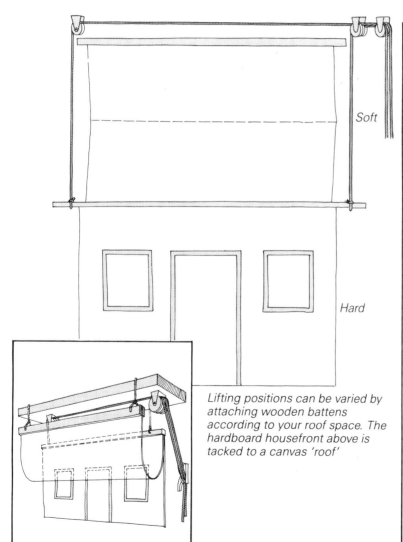

Soft

Hard

Lifting positions can be varied by attaching wooden battens according to your roof space. The hardboard housefront above is tacked to a canvas 'roof'

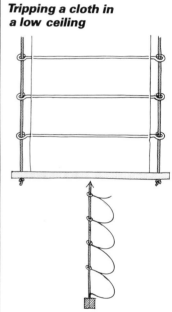

Tripping a cloth in a low ceiling

A very low ceiling can still house a cloth if the piece has several rods inserted — each being spaced the distance of the maximum lift apart. Pulleys used in tandem will enable the stage crew to lift heavier loads, but the extra roping required can be hazardous. Always tie off and tidy the excess rope immediately after the lift. Use graphite-based lubricants on timber pulleys to avoid dry squeaking and other noises

Tripping scenery

The 'olio' back-cloth

This device is valuable on stages where headroom is limited. It gives the designer flexibility to alter the scene, change the mood and accelerate scene changes. It may be purchased or hired but, if possible, should be a permanent stock item for small theaters or halls with small stages.

Making an olio

First measure the area. The cloth should be as wide as the proscenium arch, so that the back-cloth can be positioned at any point over the stage. Next measure the height of the stage and add on 1 foot (30cm) to create sufficient padding around the bottom roller.

Purchase stage canvas in as wide a form as possible to reduce the number of seams. Stitch or glue along its length and sandwich the top edge between lengths of timber 2 x 1 inches (50 x 25mm). Different methods of attaching the battens are illustrated below. These include the 'tie over' batten, 'tie through' batten and 'tie around' batten. Screw eyelets at 2 or 3 feet (90cm) intervals along this sandwich on both sides.

The bottom roller should be as light as possible and 2 feet (60cm) longer than the canvas width.

Cut circles of wood 4 inches (10cm) in diameter and lengths of wood 1 inch x 1/4 inch (25mm x 6mm) to form a long cylinder. At

each end of the roller screw on a cap made from circles of wood 6 inches x 1 inch (150mm x 25mm) to prevent the lifting rope from slipping off.

Attach rope, cable or strong webbing to the eyelets on the top of the canvas sandwich. Tie off over the main batten. Check that the top of the back-cloth is horizontal with the aid of a spirit level. Let the back-cloth hang for a while to eliminate creases. Place the bottom roller up stage of the canvas and carefully roll on the canvas. Do not tack at this stage. When the back-cloth is evenly taut, tack along its length, keeping the tension constant and the canvas smooth.

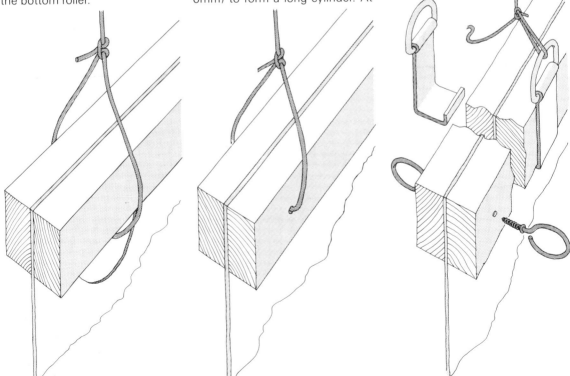

1 *Sandwich the canvas between lengths of timber batten and attach with rope or screws as above*

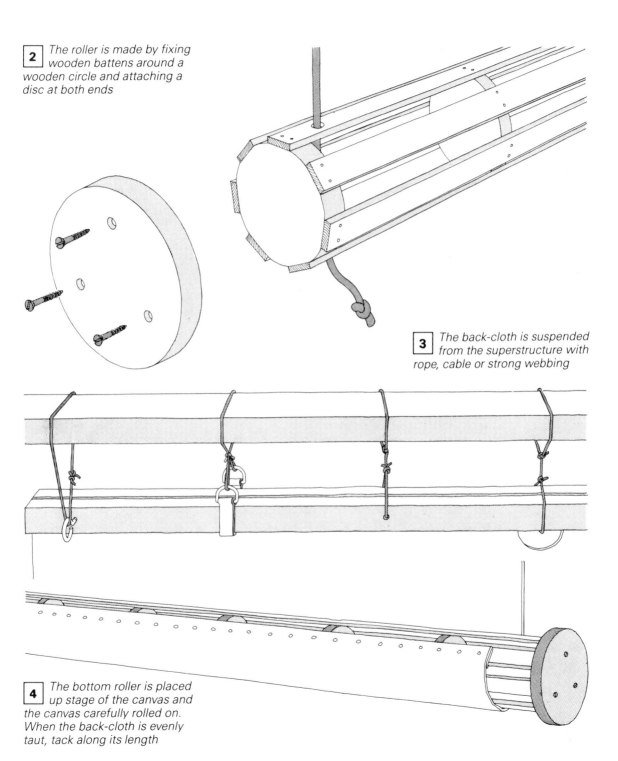

2 The roller is made by fixing wooden battens around a wooden circle and attaching a disc at both ends

3 The back-cloth is suspended from the superstructure with rope, cable or strong webbing

4 The bottom roller is placed up stage of the canvas and the canvas carefully rolled on. When the back-cloth is evenly taut, tack along its length

Gauze

Gauze lighting

Gauze is a light and closely meshed material which is semi-transparent. It is ideal for atmospheric or magical effects. When lit from the front and above, the surface is opaque but when illuminated from behind the gauze becomes transparent. It is this critical lighting angle and control which will allow you to make the most of gauze as a versatile theatrical device.

As gauze is an expensive material, experiment with the following idea before investing in a large roll. Stretch a piece of gauze over the back of a large picture frame. Secure it with a thin wooden batten. Paint a picture on the down stage face of the material. Use dyes in preference to paint as the latter can clog the mesh. Use paint only if a thicker, bolder line is required.

Set the picture frame into a door flat. Mask the gaps and use a filler flat to fill the unused space. Build a curtain box behind the flat, adding a roof if necessary so that it is light proof. Mount lighting on either side of the door flat inside the box. For a more ghostly effect position the lights below the features of the painted image.

Set the front lighting at the correct angle. Inter-connect the lights inside the box with those outside so that as one set of lights lifts the other falls.

In a play which has a ghostly or unreal element you can make use of this system with doors, alcoves and mirrors.

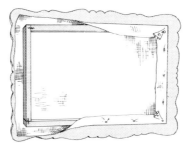

Stretch a piece of gauze over a picture frame and nail on a retaining batten

Draw your design on to the down stage face of the gauze, then paint with dyes

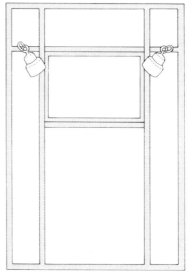

The picture frame is fitted into a door flat and then masked with a filler flat

A light-proof curtain box. Lighting is positioned on either side of the door flat

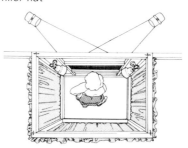

Plan of the curtain box showing lighting positions on the inside and outside

The images can appear and disappear with lighting control to create ghostly effects

Lifting the gauze

When you are confident that you can make use of the gauze technique, you can embark upon a full stage setting.

To make the transformation effective it is necessary to raise the piece of gauze smoothly and evenly. Construct an olio roller in reverse so that the gauze rolls from the top rather than the bottom. This means that the gauze can be lifted up into the ceiling in full view of the audience.

Build a 1 foot (30cm) diameter roller with as light a framework as possible, placing a pipe spindle through the center, to accommodate roping. Secure brackets at either end of the bearer bar to house the spindle. Rope with a continuous loop. The increased size of the diameter will reduce the number of revolutions required to lift the gauze, making it easier to control the speed at which it is raised. Rope in opposing turns so that as the line **A** is pulled to unwind, the other line **B** will rewind. Secure the base pulley to the stage floor.

Thread or hem a thin but rigid wire at the bottom of the gauze sheet so that its width remains constant. Grease the bracket. The extra dimension of this roller may require a deeper border to mask it. Experiment with lighting positions until you obtain the desired effect. Mask the stage floor lighting with ground rows and the overhead lights with borders and assorted cut cloth profiles.

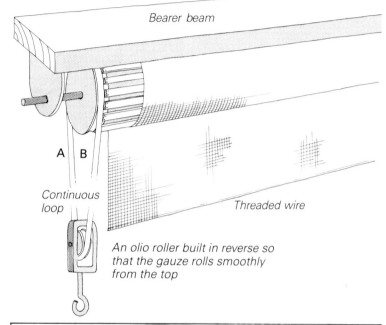

Bearer beam

A B

Continuous loop

Threaded wire

An olio roller built in reverse so that the gauze rolls smoothly from the top

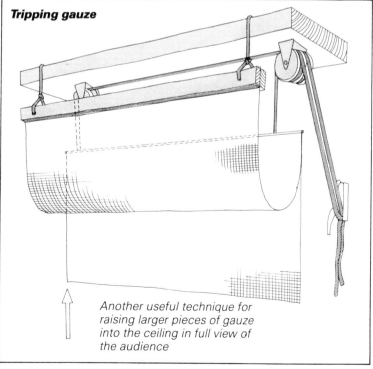

Tripping gauze

Another useful technique for raising larger pieces of gauze into the ceiling in full view of the audience

Gauze

Cut cloth settings

Stage crews always prefer soft settings to hard. They are so much easier to handle. Cut cloth profiles when used in conjunction with gauzes and ground rows give a light airy impression and are perfect for natural or ethereal settings.

To be convincing profiles need to be fragile and light. Profiles in hardboard, no matter how well painted, have an unnatural solidity and mass. You can create this quality by cutting sections out of canvas or sack cloth but if the shapes are unsupported the material will hang limply. It requires lateral and vertical stiffening. Here gauze can prevent wavering and drooping without interfering with the lightness of the effect.

Sandwich the canvas between battens and add the suspension bracket system (see page 98). Mark out and paint the design on the canvas. Using a sharp knife or blade, cut out the required areas and on the reverse side glue pieces of gauze to strengthen and maintain an even tension. Individual leaves or branches can be scattered on the gauze to increase the overall effect.

Another effective method is to hang pieces of gauze with leaf shapes glued on in a random fashion. The nature of the gauze will allow light to penetrate easily, picking out the shapes instead of the material.

Opaque paint too can be brushed on to the gauze. Choosing autumnal colors for leaves adds considerable warmth to the top of the scene without making it heavy or oppressive. In more stylized settings, foil can produce a sparkling, wintery atmosphere.

Cut cloths can also be used in short scenes or where the scenery makes only a brief appearance. Remember to stiffen where necessary with extra canvas or even wire. These require little storage space. Being soft they can also be tripped or rollered into your stage ceiling. Remember to fireproof the cloth.

1 *After painting your design on the canvas, cut out the intricate shapes using a knife*

2 *Glue pieces of gauze on to the reverse side of the canvas for strength and an even tension*

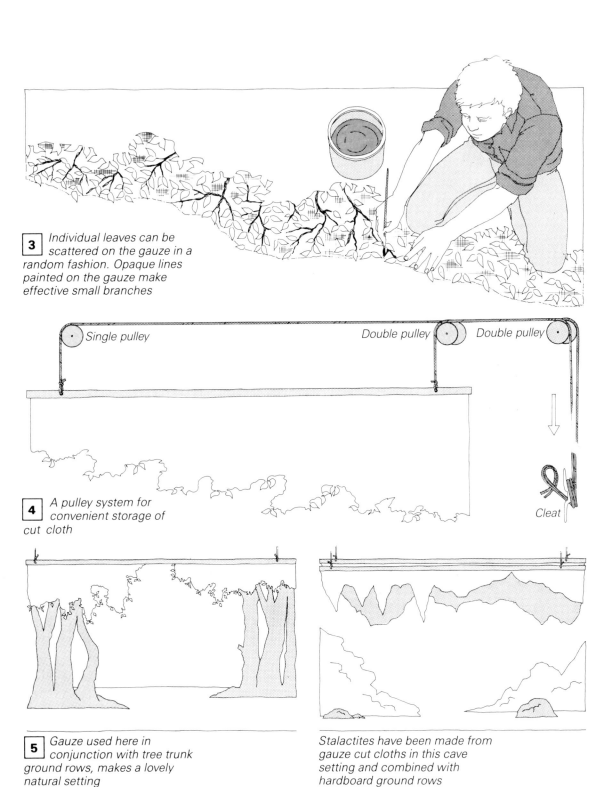

3 Individual leaves can be scattered on the gauze in a random fashion. Opaque lines painted on the gauze make effective small branches

Single pulley   Double pulley   Double pulley

Cleat

4 A pulley system for convenient storage of cut cloth

5 Gauze used here in conjunction with tree trunk ground rows, makes a lovely natural setting

Stalactites have been made from gauze cut cloths in this cave setting and combined with hardboard ground rows

Split level stages

In the past playwrights have been known to write plays with a particular theater in mind. The balcony scene in Shakespeare's *Romeo and Juliet* was played from the permanent balcony built above the stage at the Globe in London. Peter Pan flew from the well tried flying machinery of the Victorian theater.

Playwrights today, however, no longer feel so restricted. In modern drama mood, time and place can change even in mid sentence! The designer must construct a setting which can accommodate these changes without halting the flow of the scene even by the minimum amount of scenery changing.

The multi-level or split set is often the key. It can be made (if you are prepared to put in some extra effort) by the stage team on any type of stage. Structural alteration, contrasting decoration and flexible lighting patterns all play their part in the design concept, but the ability of the cast to move easily and confidently from one section of the stage to another must take priority.

If different levels are required, make them substantial and secure. This is particularly important where the stage is 'raked' i.e. sloping from up stage down towards the auditorium. Build up the down stage side with a wedge shaped platform and, if necessary, restrain it by attaching it with cables to the up stage area . If you need more height than your existing rostra can provide, use scaffolding poles which can be adjusted. Block or wire the raised floor to prevent any lateral movement. Consult a professional builder if you are in any doubt about construction.

This typical scaffold construction adds height and a variety of entrances and exits

Prevent lateral movement of the raised floor with a block or wire

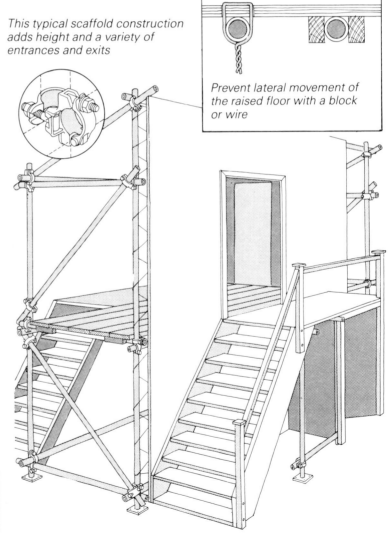

Split level on a raked stage

Scaffolding poles are adjusted so that the down stage side is built up to the right level. Cables hold the structure in position

Tiered seating in the auditorium will enable you to take full advantage of the stage level. Carpet, matting, stencil patterns or just simple paint can effectively divide the acting surface and establish particular zones. This zoning may be reinforced by strategic lighting.

Do not forget that decoration alone can change a scene. Use the stage center line to separate the different scenes. Contrasting patterns, outlines and textures of material can give you plenty of variety. For a more abstract or symbolic setting change, simply shaped rostra in the form of cubes, or cylinders may be juxtaposed.

There is always a need for a properly laid out permanent setting, especially for farce. The audience enters into the spirit of the play if it is privileged to see over walls, around corners or through closed doors.

This permanent, non scene changing arrangement has one extra bonus. It enables the stage crew to relax and see the fruits of their labour as members of the audience.

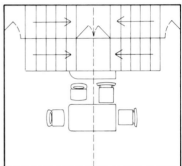

Plan view

A divided stage with contrasting arrangements of elaborate and simple furnishings

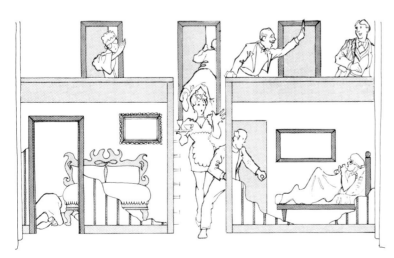

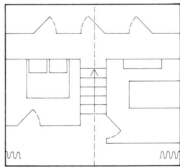

Plan view

This versatile setting enables the audience to follow the actors through doors and along corridors

Color on stage

Color is a subjective interpretation of light which is a very important aspect of set design.

The audience's response to color combination can create or destroy the atmosphere for a play. Stage lighting and costume add to this emotional response. The intensity of light and the movement and texture of costume creating harmony or discord.

The summer warmth of orange, spring-like expectancy of yellow, chillness of blue, and violence and potency of red, are just a few simple reactions with which we are all familiar. There are many subtle variations.

The secret of a successful color scheme is the confident and clever use of a few colors, or simply many shades of the same color. Skilful painting can make an object appear flatter or rounder, realistic or dreamlike, cheerful or somber.

Stage painting is a skill which can be improved with practice. Many people are frightened of the sheer size of the scenery and find it difficult to scale up both in thought and action.However once they have tasted the freedom of the greater scale — they will become enthusiastic assistants! Art departments in schools are an extra source of talent not to be ignored.

The first problem confronting a novice is the scale of the task. The second, mastering the methods of making stage paint and the third, understanding the effects which can be achieved by intelligent use and lighting of color; its hues, tones and mixtures.

Above all be bold. Work at arm's length and do not worry about being too painstaking. The audience's vision will be interrupted by properties, actors and lighting. The attention of the audience is directed towards the action of the play, not towards those small areas of unpainted canvas.

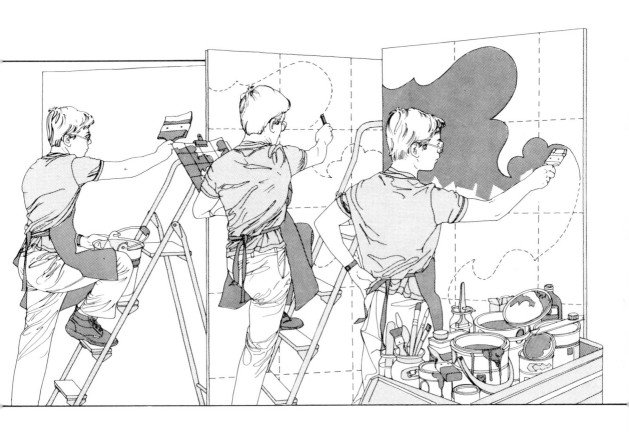

Different sources of color

The basic terminology of color needs to be known and used by the departments of lighting, wardrobe and properties, as well as make up — who suffer so often from ill disposed or wrongly colored light.

The primary colors, red, yellow and blue cannot be made by mixing. They are clear, clean and essential for a good palet. The secondary colors are those created by the mixing together of primaries, green from yellow and blue — orange from yellow and red and purple from red and blue. The process of mixing however, does tend to dull the resulting color — particularly in the case of green. Ready-made greens retain a greater brightness and intensity. The addition of white and black alters the value of all color and greatly extends the range of tone and effect.

The differences are clearly illustrated on the supplier's color cards. The pigment is supplied in paper or polythene sacks which puncture easily, so it should be transferred into glass jars and clearly labelled — the ubiquitous coffee jar is ideal. (You will always need a good supply of white and black.)

Scenic colors always dry to a lighter shade, so mix up the desired color two shades darker than you require. By painting a piece of scrap material and allowing it to dry you can test the final result.

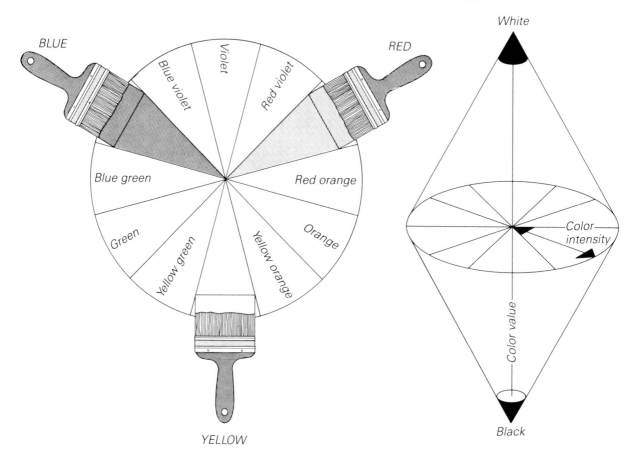

Opposite colors on the wheel contrast. If a small amount of contrasting color is added to a given hue, its intensity is reduced. Add more and you move to gray in the center of the wheel

All hues are contained within the color cone which adds a third dimension to the color wheel

The scene painter will find a selection of ready–made pigments quite adequate for most settings. The pigment colors are in powdered form. They are fixed by the addition of size — a soluble glue which binds the powder granules together. Size requires heating but emulsion glaze can be mixed in cold. Because the pigments are all intermixable, many tints and shades are possible from a small, basic stock. They are available from scenery suppliers.

Emulsion paints are very useful on separate units like ground rows or cut profiles. The body of the paint allows it to be worked and manipulated with combs and other patterned scrapers before it is dry. Mixing differing colored emulsions does not produce the predictable results gained by mixing scenic powder and although strong primaries are available, the general range is somewhat bland. Avoid the satin finish or vinyl types which are usually more expensive.

A useful 'color making' process for detailed work on separated units is the use of acrylic paints to tint and shade emulsion. No prime is needed. The strength of the color is diluted by water. (The color cannot be washed off when dry so avoid its use on your precious canvas-covered flats.) Poster color can also be used in the same way.

Light will change color value. Try to avoid too much strong pure color in any form.

Lighting color

The three basic types of stage lighting: floodlights, focus spotlights and lighting battens used with colored gelatines

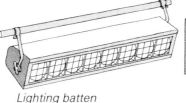

Lighting batten   *Floodlights*   *Focus spotlights*

Costume color

The red velvet of the cloak is offset by black lining material and white cotton at the throat. The clasp sparkles with silver

Pigments

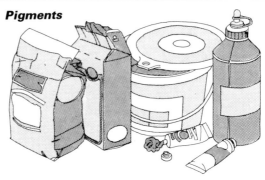

Reds: Crimson, vermilion and red

Yellows: Lemon, chrome and ochre

Blues: Ultramarine and prussian

Greens: Emerald and brunswick

Browns: Vandyke, sienna and umber ochre

White and black are available in bright and dense

Making scenic paint

A large, high–ceilinged, well lit theater workshop is ideal, but all too often this is not the case. Those groups who can paint the set after it has been made are to be envied. The most difficult situation is when limited working space prevents vertical painting, and horizontal painting is the only choice. If you are in this position, raise the flats on trestles to a more comfortable height. To prevent damage to the delicate surface of the flat, extend the trestles by adding lengths of timber which will extend beyond the stiles. A wheeled trolley upon which the various cans of paint, brushes and other equipment may be carried is very helpful.

Scenic paint reaches the right consistency with the addition of size. This dissolves only in warm water so a ready supply of heat and water should be near at hand. An old camping cooker, an electric hotplate or a gas ring will serve so lóng as the heat is quickly controllable. You will need a variety of buckets, plastic containers and other leak-proof containers as well as an assortment of rags and cloths. Old metal trays make ersatz pallets when painting small areas. Rather than waiting till the actual moment when these various items are needed it is wise to encourage all members of the group to save any useful odds and ends. Old shirts are very useful when making paint or painting scenery.

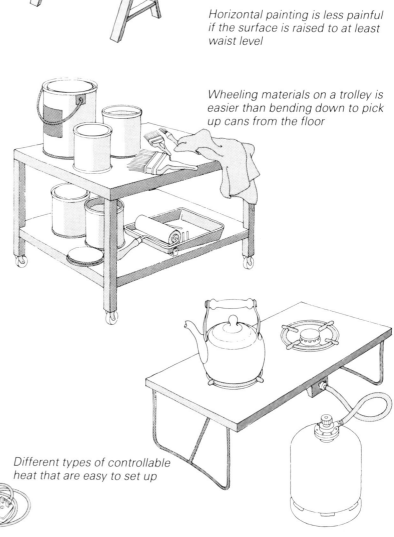

Horizontal painting is less painful if the surface is raised to at least waist level

Wheeling materials on a trolley is easier than bending down to pick up cans from the floor

Different types of controllable heat that are easy to set up

Making stage whiting

This is a basic primer for preparing canvas. The priming coat should be applied with a large brush or roller. If the setting is to be in a light color, use this basic whiting. Settings with a strong color may need color added at the priming stage. (Canvas covered by many layers of paint should have the surface washed and scraped off before re-priming).Make up the size in a bucket — one part size — one part water. Stir and allow the 'porridge' to soak. Add six or seven pints (4 ls) of boiling water to the paste, stirring thoroughly until the concentrate is fully dissolved.

Half fill a similar bucket with stage whiting. Cover it with cold water. Soak overnight to eliminate any lumps. Reheat the size, add this slowly to the whiting, stirring continuously. Mix in size until you have a thin, creamy consistency. Test its covering power by test card. It should remain opaque when dry.

The procedure is the same when making up stage paint. After the size has been dissolved it is mixed with the pigment powder to bind the color and prevent dusting and flaking of the scenic paint. Half size to paint is the normal proportion, made up as shown opposite. Remember, scenic color dries lighter so mix in more dark mixed pigment to produce the correct tone. Test the thin, creamy mixture on a test card and compare it with the original color sketches of the set and the material used for costumes.

1 Make up the size in a bucket — one part size to one part cold water. Stir and allow it to soak

2 Add 6 or 7 pints (4 ls) of boiling water to the paste. Stir until dissolved

3 Half fill another bucket with stage whiting. Cover it with cold water and leave to soak

4 Reheat the size and add it slowly to the whiting, stirring continuously till thin and creamy

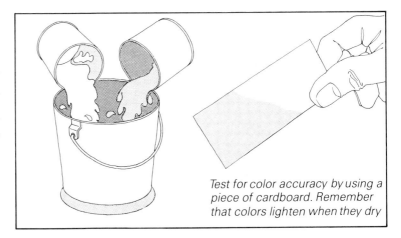

Test for color accuracy by using a piece of cardboard. Remember that colors lighten when they dry

Brushes and painting aids

Scenery painting involves a broad and confident approach. The scale and technique of painting — from the acreage of single color 'laying in' to the finer brushwork on separate pieces — is a large step to take even for someone used to painting in a conventional way. A certain element of flair is needed and young art students respond to the challenge. Recruit them at every opportunity.

A wide variety of brushes certainly makes the adjustment easier. They are readily available — albeit in a wide price range according to quality. Make certain that time and money are not wasted by taking good care of all painting aids. Replacement is always expensive. Insist that after every session, everyone from the skilled painter to the enthusiastic amateur makes time to clean the brushes very thoroughly.

Covering large surfaces ('laying in') is best achieved by using wide bristle brushes. A 5 or 6 inch (15cm) brush suits the purpose well. For small areas use pure or mixed bristle brushes from 1 inch to 3 inches (25-75mm).

A variety of fitches are necessary for detailed work. These are brushes with a relatively small head and a long stock. The brush head can be square, angled or round. The effect required on stage rarely needs anything smaller than half an inch (12mm) to complete the job.

A painter's mahl-stick is, when fully mastered, a very useful aid. Simply tie a ball of cloth to one end of a 3 feet (90cm) rod or bamboo. With practice you will be able to paint controlled straight lines on to a vertical surface like a commercial signwriter.

Hold the rod in your non painting hand. Place the padded end against the dry surface of the flat. Rest the heel of the hand or wrist on the support provided and apply the required pressure to the brush head. Straight lines and curves may now be approached with less shake and more confidence!

Lined sections may be painted on horizontal planes with the aid of a straight-edge. Before using tack a piece of 1 inch (25mm) batten on to the underside of the straight-edge to keep it away from the surface to be painted. Hold the ferrule of the brush against the straight-edge and draw the brush towards you, exerting the necessary pressure.

The height of flats takes them beyond the reach of even the tallest painter. A good stepladder, 6 feet (180 cm) high should cope with most situations. A hollow tube, wide enough to hold the

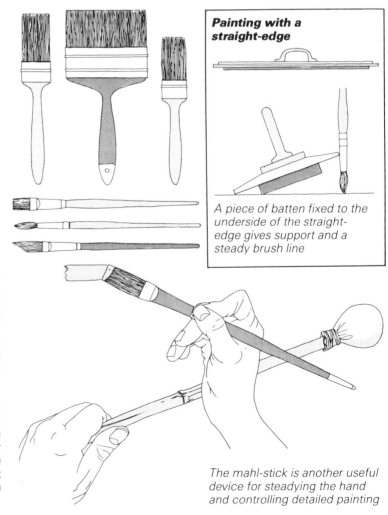

Painting with a straight-edge

A piece of batten fixed to the underside of the straight-edge gives support and a steady brush line

The mahl-stick is another useful device for steadying the hand and controlling detailed painting

brush handle is useful when last minute touching up is required, and all other devices have been stored away.

If you are fortunate enough to be able to paint the scenery after it has been erected, make sure that the floor surface is protected before you begin painting. Old curtains or plastic sheeting are excellent. Because so much painting is above eye level it is wise to wear either old clothes or a painting overall, and a cap.

Masking tape is a simple and effective way of creating straight colored lines or to divide color areas. Commercial tape is quite expensive and ordinary cellophane tape is a good substitute. First paint on the color you wish to reveal and allow it to dry, then press the tape down firmly to avoid bleeding and apply the main body coat. When this is dry — peel off the tape to expose a straight, even line of contrasting or complimentary color.

A snap-line is a length of cord covered thoroughly with chalk. By stretching the line tautly over the surface, securing at both ends then 'plucking' the cord with finger and thumb, the line will snap back on to the surface, leaving a deposit of chalk behind. Strengthen the line with charcoal. This technique is useful when you need to scale up a drawing.

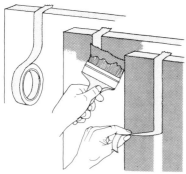

Masking tape peeled off after the top coat has dried, reveals even bands of the base color

A stepladder and 'extended brush' — useful for work above shoulder height

A snap-line deposits a guiding chalk line on to large areas

Brush techniques

To avoid the starkness of a single tone and to create warmth and depth, various brush handling techniques are useful, and easily mastered.

One of the simplest of these is wet blending. Using a separate wide brush for each can, two or three colors are brushed or blended together whilst still wet. This works best on a broad scale.

Dry brushing is another blending method based on the same principle. Only the tip of each brush is covered in paint and this is drawn lightly over the surface in a random fashion to give a feathery soft effect.

Spattering is simply a flicking action of the wrist. The brush does not touch the surface but showers droplets of paint. Several different colors can be applied in this way. Beware — spattering can get out of control — non painters should stand well clear! The principle of multiple tones applies here as in all painting techniques.

Scumbling means twisting and turning the brush to produce an uneven texture. The paint should be thick enough to create a raised swirling movement with each blending stroke.

One of those old, worn, unwashed brushes can be given a new lease of life with the stippling technique. Apply different pressure to produce dotted and spotted areas. Together with contrasting colors this produces a most interesting surface texture. The color should be fairly dry and the brush never overloaded — only the irregular tips need touch the surface.

Wet blending

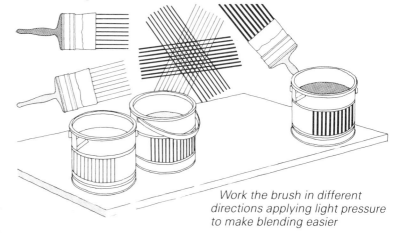

Work the brush in different directions applying light pressure to make blending easier

Dry brushing

Draw the brush tip lightly over the base to give a feathering effect

Spattering

A supple wrist is all that is required for this painting action

Scumbling

Twist and turn the brush energetically to swirl the paint

Stippling and dabbing

Small quantities of paint are dabbed and pressed on

Wood graining and glazing

The movement and overlaying of paint is similar to the previous techniques but to produce a realistic reproduction you should make a close study of the actual grained surface of wood. The tendency is to paint knot effects everywhere.

The right brushwork is crucial. Increasingly darker tones are wet blended together, and the grain direction is defined with smaller brushes. Use the stock end of the brush to draw or comb lines into the wet surface. If the effect is required on a door, or other hard surface, and not on a canvas flat, an emulsion glaze can provide a convincing polished effect.

Marbling

This can look pleasingly realistic but it requires practice and you will have to expect the occasional failure. Paint the surface with white and allow it dry. Using a thinner white paint cover the area to be marbled and while this is still wet, paint irregular brown and ochre lines diagonally across the surface using a small artist's brush. Dry brush over the lines to smudge them. Using a darker brown tint repeat the line-drawing and smudging process and allow the surface to dry. Polish with wax polish or, if painting in emulsion, use the vinyl type.

Marbled paper is useful for covering smaller areas. Half-fill a bowl or photographic tray with water and a little wallpaper paste. Add oil-based paint and stir to create a pattern. Bring the paper briefly into contact with the surface and then hang it up to dry.

Wood graining

Base color is applied.

A darker tone is blended over this

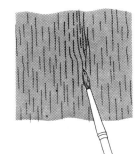

Lines are added with a thinner brush over the blended colors

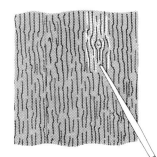

Using the stock end of a brush, comb lines into the wet paint

Marbling

Paint a thin coat of white over the existing dry white surface

A variety of umber lines are painted on the still wet surface

Lines are then dry brushed to smudge the original line

Darker brown and ochre lines are then re-drawn

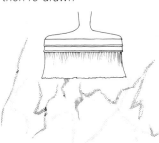

Dry-brush once more and polish the surface with wax

Paint rollers

The paint roller is now widely used for general decorating around the home and has provided the scenic artist with another labor saving device and some clever design innovations.

When buying a roller bear the following points in mind, so that you choose the best suited to your task. Some rollers have hollow handles to which you can add a broom handle. This will enable you to paint the topmost areas of a flat without resorting to stepladders. If flats are painted in a horizontal position it will mean less strain on your back and avoid damage to the flat's surface.

Roller surface textures vary considerably from man-made sponge to sheepskin and suede. The more expensive rollers are more efficient at covering large areas, but the cheaper variety are quite suitable for adapting to alternative uses. The roller is held on to the spindle by a retaining nut allowing you to change or replace the roller with ease.

Stage lighting on vertical flats creates areas of highlight and shadow. By adding progressively darker tones over the main base color you can assist this effect without increasing the lighting on the set. Do not completely cover the base color. Allow each layer of color to show through.

This method of overlaying color to produce texture is well illustrated by the technique of reproducing stone or brickwork. Make up a variety of related colors and apply each with a separate roller, obscuring totally the underlying colors. Manipulating the direction of the roller reproduces the different shapes of stone or brick as well as the differing tones.

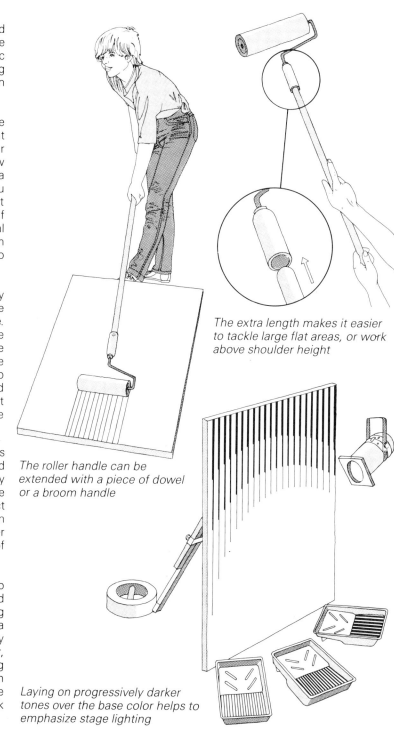

The extra length makes it easier to tackle large flat areas, or work above shoulder height

The roller handle can be extended with a piece of dowel or a broom handle

Laying on progressively darker tones over the base color helps to emphasize stage lighting

Stonework or brickwork effect

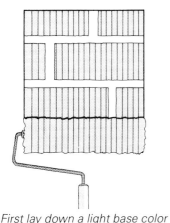

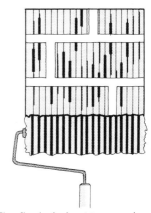

First lay down a light base color and paint on mortar joints

Patches of darker color add more depth and texture

The final, darkest tone makes the surface appear uneven

Cut rollers

Using a scalpel or razor, cut away sections of a cheap roller leaving a raised design. The cut pattern can be symmetrical or in the case of leaves, irregularly arranged. By rolling in different directions with different colors a fascinating variety of surface textures are possible.

The effect of foliage is built up gradually, starting with a dark tone and finally adding subtle highlights. Do clean the roller between each color change.

It is difficult to avoid a fine spray caused by the movement of the roller so whenever you use it, protect your clothing and surrounding areas.

Rag rolling

Wrap a rag around the roller and tie it on with string. Make up a creamy consistency of paint in the roller tray and lightly apply this to the flat's surface. The irregularity of the folds of the rag will create interesting tones.

A similar technique can be applied by taping the roller with masking tape. Overlay different colors and tones as well as changing the roller direction. The resultant texture helps break down an unrelieved uniform surface.

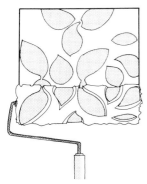

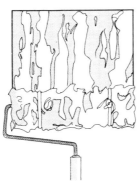

Cut out shapes from the roller surface for a more intricately worked design

A rag is tied around the roller and the folds make patterned 'wallpaper' or 'bark'

Masking tape fixed to the roller for painting straight lines or dividing colored areas

Textured surfaces

Textured surfaces need careful positioning on stage. Lit from the side the roughness of the surface and the interplay of light and shadow are shown to their best advantage.

Bear in mind that the time and cost involved in this process may not always justify the effort. A piece of scenery with a textured surface can rarely be recovered, or used in future productions.

Textured surfaces add weight to scenery, and will not stand too much handling or movement. Use them in a permanent setting where the design is based on color and texture rather than constructed scenery.

Wood chippings and sawdust shavings

This is a very good use of the raw material which is readily available from the stage workshop or any woodworking business. Brush glue or heavy size on to the horizontal hard surface. Sprinkle sawdust or shavings on top and leave it to dry. When gluing larger wood chips place a weighted board over the pieces and apply pressure to ensure that good contact is made with the more irregular shapes.

Creating a textured surface with wood shavings

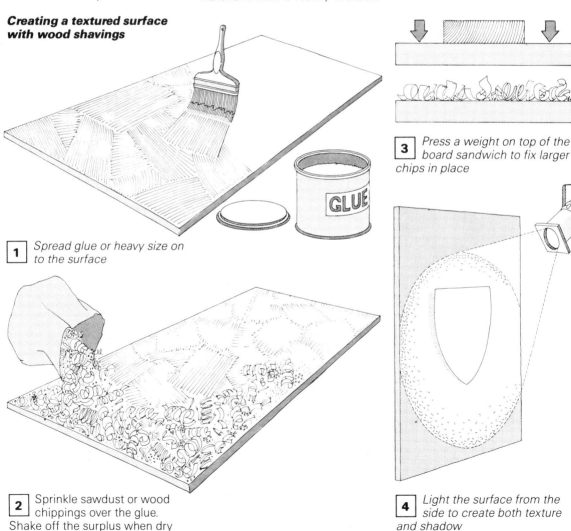

1 *Spread glue or heavy size on to the surface*

2 Sprinkle sawdust or wood chippings over the glue. Shake off the surplus when dry

3 *Press a weight on top of the board sandwich to fix larger chips in place*

4 *Light the surface from the side to create both texture and shadow*

118

Plastering with paint

Commercially produced heavy textured paint is excellent for this technique. It is applied thickly and, before drying out, it can be worked with a cardboard comb or shaped instrument. Different shaped effects are achieved depending on the size and spacing of the comb teeth. The comb can be pivoted or dragged downwards for a circular or fluted effect. Details such as woodgrain knots may be added afterwards with a nail. Paint is longer lasting and more adhesive than plaster, but you can create the same surface 'movement'.

Comb a pattern on to the thick paint before it is dry

Offcuts of paper or cloth

Soak old newsprint or scrap paper in size, or fold it roughly and apply it in this crinkled form to the prepared surface. Undercoat with white emulsion paint and spray or sponge on color. This method is a useful way of texturing ground rows or panels.

Soak pieces of paper or cloth in size and arrange on a board

Paint on an undercoat of white emulsion and spray or sponge on color afterwards

Timber scraps

Pieces of timber or hardboard are glued and tacked to a firmly supported old flat to make interesting shapes for both texture and shadow. Foil too can be arranged in a similar fashion.

Arrange unusual shapes of wood to make a collage. Paint in different colors if required

Wallpaper

Wallpapering of course will provide instant pattern and texture. Large patterns are much more effective than small, but should not be too prominent. A wallpaper effect can also be achieved by blocking with polystyrene or by stencil. The grading of tone by these methods makes them far more exciting and original than standard commercial wallpapers.

Polystyrene sheeting

Take fire precautions with this material. However, covered with muslin and thinly plastered, it is adaptable and easily shaped.

Stenciling and blocking

The principle of repetitive patterning is well established in the design process. These patterns can be achieved by stencil or simple block printing.

To be effective, the pattern should be quite large and relatively uncomplicated. Stenciling for the larger areas required on stage relies on the stencil paper being strong, thick and waterproof to prevent the pattern disintegrating under the less than gentle handling it will receive. It may even be trampled upon!

Frame the stencil with thick cardboard. Mark out the pattern edge line with a plumb-line and chalk on the surface to be stenciled. Cut register marks on the stencil frame. Apply color by stippling or sponging with thick drier paint (see page 114).

Stenciling

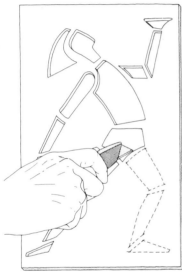

1 *Cut out the pattern from stencil cardboard. Make sure that the shapes are not connected*

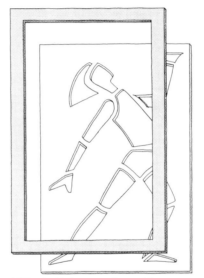

2 *A thicker cardboard frame protects the stencil from damage. Mark the pattern edge with a plumb-line*

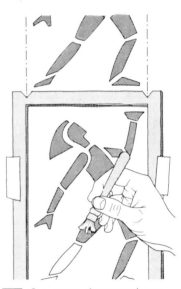

3 *Cut out register marks on the stencil frame. Place the stencil in position and block in the color*

On thrust or arena stages where other scenery is at a minimum and the stage surface is visible to the audience, a pattern on the stage can be attractive and practical. Used at the edge to signify a wall it may just register on the actor's eye to prevent him falling off!

If you are tempted to use a paint spray, protect the other exposed surfaces before beginning.

Stencil decoration makes a convincing wall at the edge of the stage, and also prevents the actors from walking too far!

Block printing is unsuitable for anything less than the tautest of surfaces. The pattern must be in bas-relief, polystyrene sheets are suitable — the pattern can be 'pokered', or cut out with a blade.

Polystyrene is both easily melted and extremely fragile. If you plan to use the block extensively, it is best to mount the polystyrene first on to a block of plywood.

Draw out the design with a flow pen. Paint over the parts of the design to be printed and hold over a flame to melt the polystyrene not covered with paint. Alternatively use a hot wire or poker to trace the lines. Draw register marks on the reverse side of the plywood. Use a roller to lay paint on to the design and press down upon the plywood to make a print.

Blocking

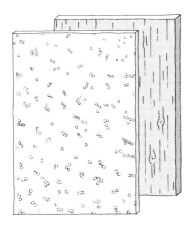

1 *Glue a sheet of polystyrene to plywood or hardboard and draw out a design with a flow pen*

2 *Paint the parts to be printed with thick paint. Use a hot wire or poker to trace the lines, or*

3 *pass the polystyrene quickly over a naked flame to melt the sections not covered with paint*

4 *Roll the paint evenly over the surface of the block. Recharge with paint to maintain density*

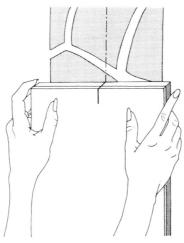

5 *Press the block down firmly using the register mark to line up the pattern correctly*

'Stonework' repeat pattern

Glue spaced pieces of polystyrene on to a board. Roll on the color and press hard when printing

Scaling up

The standard scale used in the professional theater is ¼ inch (6mm) to 1 foot (30cm). The generally smaller proportions of amateur stages, however, make this unrealistic for both drawings and models. A scale of ½ inch (12mm) to 1 foot (30cm) is more manageable.

To enlarge a scale model or finished drawing of a back-cloth to actual size, simply square up the drawing or elevation of the model to your chosen measurement. Repeat the squaring process on the cloth or scenery flat in the related scale. (See page 38). A snap-line is the most effective and simple method of transferring the grid scale.

Number and letter the corresponding squares, 1A, 1B and so on.

If the canvas is laid upon the floor, push a stick of charcoal into the hollow end of a bamboo stick. The charcoal extension will help you reach the top. Make key marks before embarking on the drawing out process. The direction and angle of line can easily be related to the scaling lines.

Using a snap-line to transfer the grid scale. Number and letter corresponding squares

Atmospheric painting

The sky-cloth or back-cloth is the largest single area on stage. It is directly in the audience's line of vision and as such will do much to determine the mood of the play.

To produce good results your work place should aim for a similar lighting intensity to that used on your stage.

The paintings of the French Impressionists will guide not only your color selection but also brushwork technique and juxtaposition of color and form. Their execution was based on close observation of nature, and Nature is still your best guide when interpreting distance.

All colors are changed by atmosphere. As the eye travels toward the horizon, the sky changes and the landscape takes on tones of blue. Use a free brushing technique to portray this and avoid dense, opaque areas of color. Allow the white undercoat to show through — its presence creates sparkle.

Landscape involves line and planes. Distance is enhanced by the interplay of both these features. The eye is drawn into the distance and then returns to the foreground quite predictably. Aid its return by gradually increasing color, strength and detail.

When painting a back-cloth there is a great tempation to paint dramatic cloud formations for the pure pleasure of it. Beware — the script may indicate something entirely different! The real sky is perpetually changing, so it is better by far to paint an even graded tone upon which the lighting engineers can play a variety of lighting effects. When striving for an effect on large areas, break off from painting frequently to view from the auditorium. If this is not possible, squint through half-closed eyes from a short distance. This will give you the overall effect which is easily lost if you are working too close to the canvas. An extension handle will allow a freer approach.

It is important to reflect accurately the landscape of the period in which the play is set. Hedgerows and field formations are a trap for the unwary. Research details of architecture and building so that you paint in the correct materials and outlines.

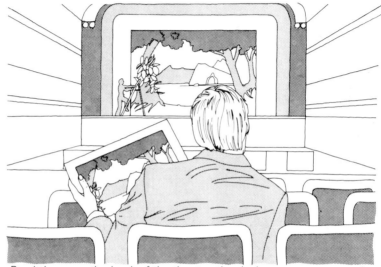

By sitting near the back of the theater, the designer can compare the original sketch with the work in progress, and adjust the color tones to achieve the right atmosphere

The eye is naturally drawn towards the horizon in the distance. Use of detail and tone will draw it back to the foreground

Illusionary painting techniques

The eye is easily distracted and consequently deceived by the clever use of shadow — the mouth line of the Mona Lisa is a perfect example. The lack of hard defined lines will allow the mind to see what it wishes or expects to see. Here are a few examples of the tricks which can be played on the uninitiated eye.

The need to decorate plain flats, to interrupt the bland featureless expanse of canvas, is part of the scene painter's task. If cleverly painted, relief effect can be obtained quite simply — panelled doors, picture frames, molding and architraves can be quite convincing.

Molding or architraves

It is important when marking out the decoration, that parallel lines remain parallel, and vertical lines remain vertical. Take care to mark out the lines accurately with a snap-line, spirit level and plumb-line before painting. Do all measuring from the stage floor level upwards rather than from the top of flats.

Before painting, identify the main light source. Mix ample base tone, shade tone, and light tint. Select a narrow fitch liner. You will also need the mahl-stick for supporting your painting hand (see page 112).

Door panel

First paint the light tint along the 'surface' facing the light and then add the shade tone. The width of the shadow line may become wider as it moves away from a fixed light source. On door panelling the 'shadows' cast by the bottom panels are slightly darker than those at eye level.

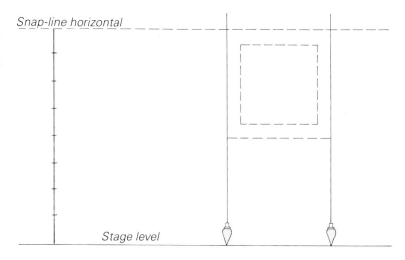

Snap-line horizontal

Stage level

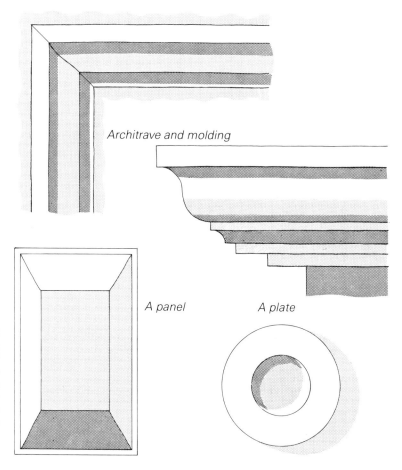

Architrave and molding

A panel

A plate

Depth illusion

When extra depth is required for alcoves or shelves, simply paint extra shadow under the shelf on the back face of the unit. Highlighting any piece standing on the shelf will help the illusion. If lit from above, the bottom shelf will be in deepest shadow. Avoid plain black, mix blue and black or brown and black instead. Although the resultant tone is dull it avoids the deadness often produced by pure black.

Used in conjunction with a row of book spines a very narrow alcove can be made to look quite deep.

Broken edges

Simple flats present a very uniform and rigid vertical line when used as hard masking. Use black to eat into that line to accentuate the surface you have applied, such as bricks or weatherboard and stonework. Add shading along the horizontal line also.

This type of detailed painting can make all the difference to the success of the illusion you are trying to create.

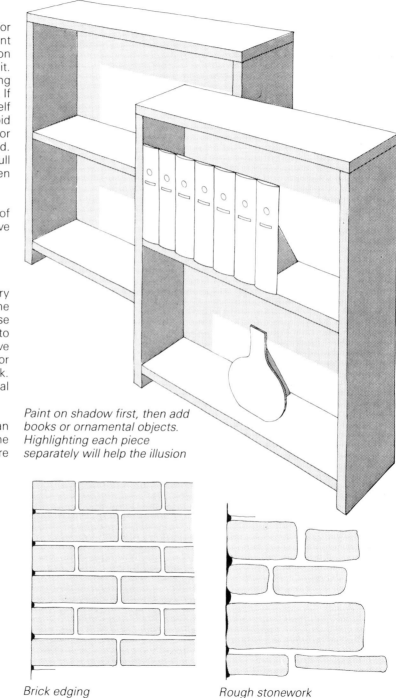

Paint on shadow first, then add books or ornamental objects. Highlighting each piece separately will help the illusion

Weatherboarding

Brick edging

Rough stonework

Theater options

The strutting players of Shakespeare's *Hamlet* and Judy Garland's plaintive *Born in a Trunk* are good illustrations of the way actors have been obliged to seek out potential audiences. They work 'on the road' constantly and spend a considerable part of their working lives in theatrical lodgings.

The changing pattern of entertainment, and the increasing amount of passive television and video viewing at home have lessened the demand for live theater. Rising production costs and seat prices have also combined to stop theater-going being, as it once was, a universally popular pastime.

However, the local flavor of amateur theater presents a viable alternative. Adventurous presentation and improving standards can attract audiences and provide what may well be the only opportunity to see live theater at affordable prices. This means that a pale imitation of a well known, well worn 'pot-boiler' may not prove to be a crowd puller. It has probably been shown recently in black and white as the late night movie!

Build into your program a variety of productions, and an element of unpredictability. The media have created a taste for novelty and change. By gaining a reputation for innovation your group will benefit. The following sections cover alternative ways you can make the most of your theater and cast. The advice is based on actual experience of design and production and is applied to some common situations and problems.

If necessary go beyond your playhouse walls to seek inspiration. Go back on the road. It will certainly pose some problems but the necessary involvement of every section of the group will combine to find a solution. The experience you will gain by this sort of adventure can only serve you well in future productions, and possibly increase your membership and finances.

Street theater

The early Christian Church, although originally highly censorious of the theater, gradually accepted the power of drama as a means of communicating with the people. It steadily transformed pagan festivals into Christian Saint plays and religious feasts.

Eventually the Church, the city corporations and the craft guilds joined forces to build and decorate wagons which could be driven through the narrow streets. In time the range of stories widened and the spoken language changed from Latin to English.

Nowadays street theater is used as a vehicle for many causes, and the summer season of fairs and fêtes provides an ideal opportunity for your group to participate.

In the open air, speech needs to be uncomplicated. Setting the play on a truck or flat wagon requires the simplest of scenery. All you need is a back curtain and an entrance through it, steps to ground level and the simplest of ground rows or profiles.

Because street theater is usually part of a wider festival the talents and resources of the whole neighborhood can be tapped. Bands or music groups from local schools, scaffolding and materials from local builders and, possibly, horses and ponies from a nearby equestrian center may be hired. The dance center may also welcome the opportunity to join in and perform.

Although the set construction for this type of presentation is very straightforward, the overall conception needs careful attention to establish the right atmosphere.

The stability of the acting surface and access to it is important.

Suspend a 'ceiling' over the stage. Make it of light material so that it does not flap noisily and allows light through it. Muslin is ideal and it also helps the voice to project. If necessary a well disguised microphone may help to defeat competing noise from the surrounding fair.

Plays do not have to be religious, but a stylized version of Good versus Evil is a good basis. Your audience will be of many ages, so do not forget the children, who love to join in. The overall aim is to provide color, sound and entertainment. Use the opportunity to advertise your forthcoming production!

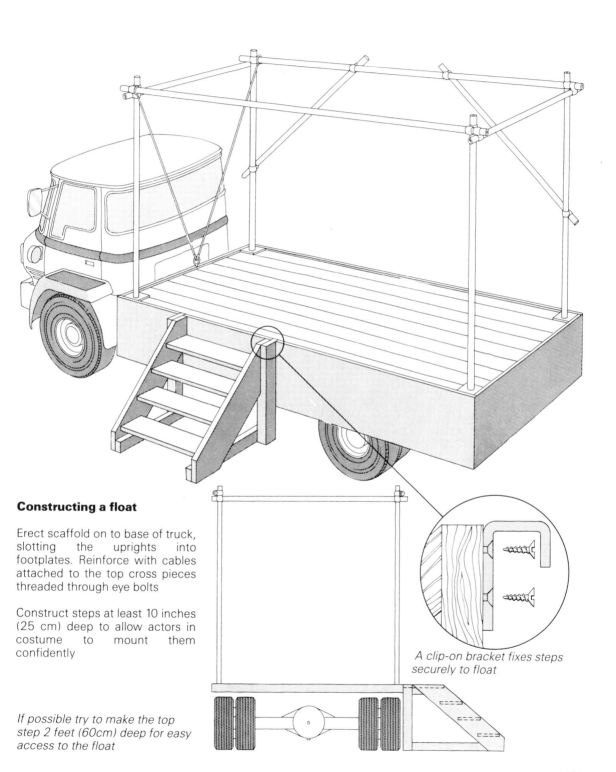

Constructing a float

Erect scaffold on to base of truck, slotting the uprights into footplates. Reinforce with cables attached to the top cross pieces threaded through eye bolts

Construct steps at least 10 inches (25 cm) deep to allow actors in costume to mount them confidently

If possible try to make the top step 2 feet (60cm) deep for easy access to the float

A clip-on bracket fixes steps securely to float

Street theater

Constructing a scaffold stage

A raised platform is essential to gain the attention of the crowd in a presentation out of doors. Use a spirit level at all times to ensure that the construction is both safe and level. The audience views from many angles, so avoid side curtains unless for decoration

Position the colored curtaining at the back of the scaffold, allowing for an entrance. Thread the pole through a hem or pin securely.

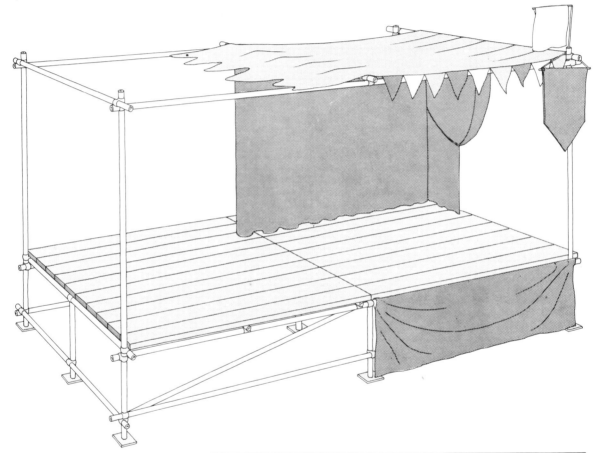

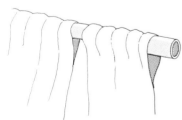

Curtains are attached by threading the pole through a hem or pinning securely

A muslin ceiling

Use muslin as a stage ceiling. It is very lightweight, stretches easily and is semi-transparent.

It will provide both cover, and a sounding board. You may need to re-stretch it to retain a tight surface. Make the hem/sleeve to fit the pole structure

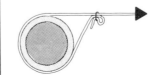

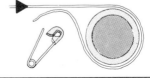

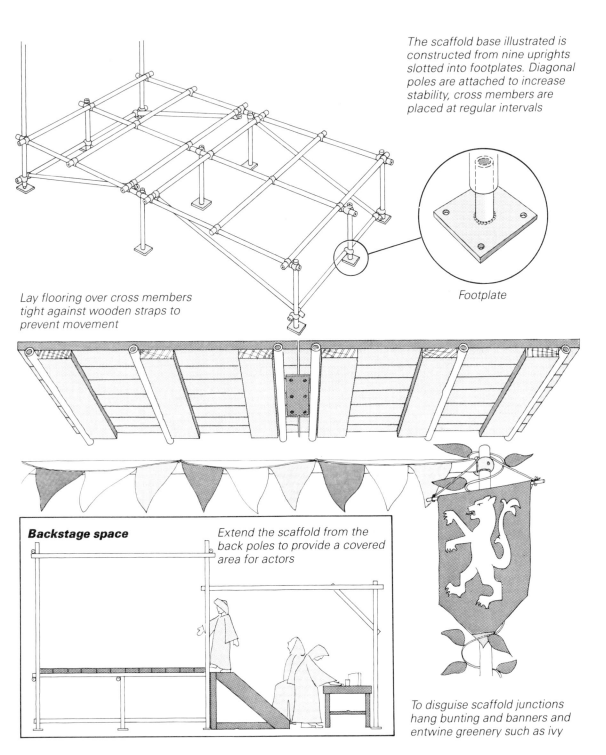

The scaffold base illustrated is constructed from nine uprights slotted into footplates. Diagonal poles are attached to increase stability, cross members are placed at regular intervals

Footplate

Lay flooring over cross members tight against wooden straps to prevent movement

Backstage space

Extend the scaffold from the back poles to provide a covered area for actors

To disguise scaffold junctions hang bunting and banners and entwine greenery such as ivy

Street theater

Building a Punch and Judy booth

The original Punch and Judy gave pleasure to children of all ages and a 'live' version can easily be presented using this lightweight portable booth. Its bright red and yellow stripes will always attract attention, and the format can be used for short, satirical sketches.

Using 1½ inch (38mm) x ½ inch (12mm) battens make two wing flats and a proscenium. Use butt joints with corrugated fasteners reinforced by triangular plywood plates glued and tacked. Make the wings 1 inch (25mm) narrower than half the front for easy folding. Position the hinges so that the wings butt up to the back of the proscenium.

Screw two large hooks just below the rear top edge of the wing to hold a lightweight back-cloth. Paint, or get a child to paint, a simple landscape on a sized piece of cotton sheet. (See **Drama for younger children**.)

Top and bottom braces are secured to the wing section by screw or dowel so that they swing back when not in use.

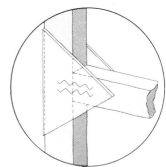

Use corrugated fasteners with triangular plates

Screw a large hook close to the top of each wing flat

Position hinges so that the 'wing' butts up to the proscenium

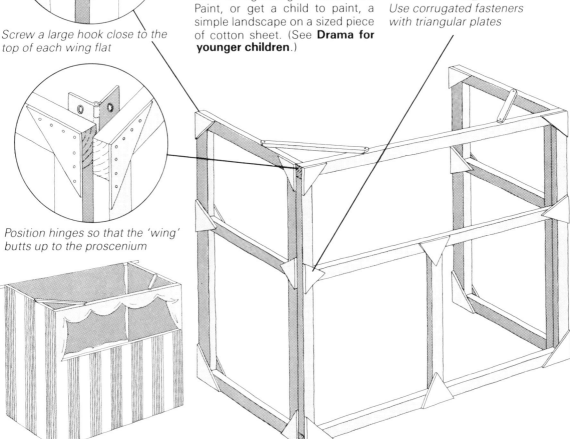

A canvas banqueting table

This is simply a length of canvas fixed to a long pole. Token dishes, plates, and flasks are painted in boldly and outlined in black.

Unroll to reveal an instant 'banqueting table'.

This method can be adapted to suit almost any piece of scenery which does not remain on the scaffold for too long.

To build a throne

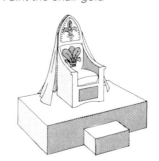

Cut out simple profiles and nail them to an existing chair. Paint the chair gold

Use box rostra to create a permanent high level at the back of the acting surface

Revue

The term 'revue' is used to cover a multitude of theater forms from lavish spectacle to satire, from Las Vegas opulence to seaside summer show.

It was first used in the last century to describe a loose sequence of sketches, songs and monologues which commented upon contemporary events.

The format was later adapted to include music and glittering parades of dancing girls interspersed with comedy acts but with no discernible theme or story line.

It is not this expensive 'quasi musical' approach which best suits the amateur but more the intimate type of revue which concentrates more on wit and pace and less on rich costume and dancing. Noel Coward, Gertrude Lawrence and Beatrice Lillie were among the fine high comedy performers who helped develop this genre. More recently a satirical and less tuneful aspect has been introduced.

As a consequence of this varied development, there is a wealth of ready made material. Although in many cases it is somewhat dated, it can guide your group's scriptwriters in the right direction.

It takes a considerable amount of time and patience to produce suitable material and the foreplanning stage of a production must be greatly extended to allow for editing material and integrating it into the show plan. The acts need careful timing and dovetailing so that the joins do not show.

The stage settings should be uncomplicated to help sustain the pace of the performance. Back-cloths, or front cloths, lightweight properties and profiles, ample costume changing room close to the performing area, will help to move a revue along without embarrassing pauses.

The keys to a fast moving show, are soft masking and fleet-footed performers!

Soft masking or leg curtains allow the crew to remove bulky or awkwardly shaped scenery and props swiftly. Agile performers are preferred because they can avoid those same bulky units and still get on stage before their introductory music or 'seque' has ended. Revue rarely calls for large numbers on stage at any one time and consequently some four feet (120cm) of the up stage area may be reserved for stage mounted floodlights and ground rows which act as camouflage. These can be interchanged for different acts leaving the lighting to set the mood. With a little planning beforehand, you can save time with construction and scene changing. Simply place differently shaped hardboard sections in sequence on the down stage side.

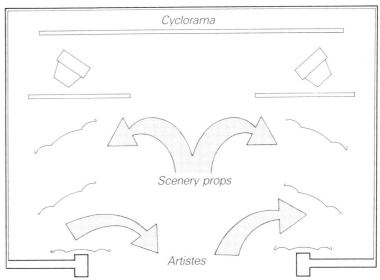

Pre-determine the entrance and exits of both artistes and scenery. Try to avoid collisions by designating a separate route for each

Interchanging ground rows

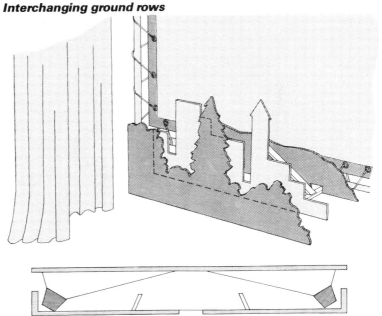

Soft masking

A large trucked unit is discreetly moved through a 'scenery' exit

A good proportion of the up stage area is reserved for stage mounted floods, and ground rows. The different sections are moved down stage to change the scene

Revue

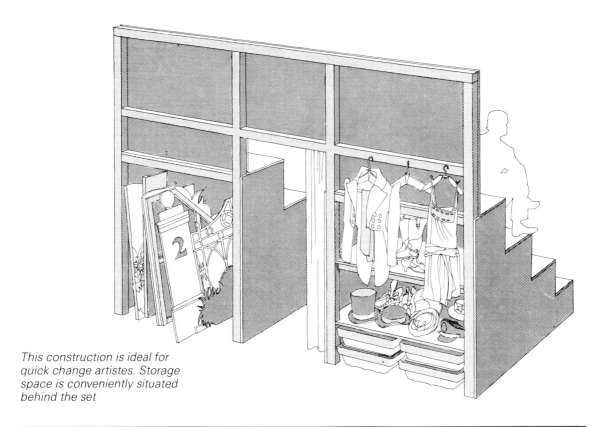

This construction is ideal for
quick change artistes. Storage
space is conveniently situated
behind the set

Stable doors for a variety of
entrances and 'one-liners' and
a wider curtained arch for more
complicated acts

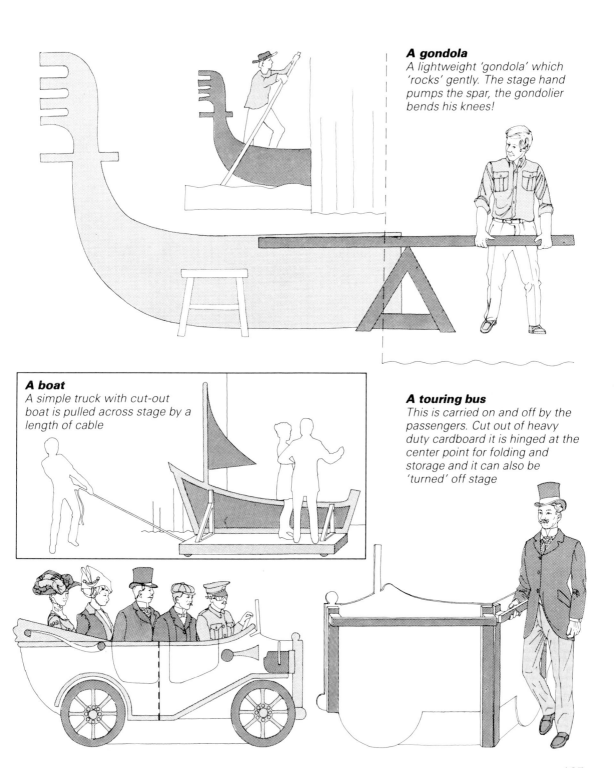

A gondola

A lightweight 'gondola' which 'rocks' gently. The stage hand pumps the spar, the gondolier bends his knees!

A boat

A simple truck with cut-out boat is pulled across stage by a length of cable

A touring bus

This is carried on and off by the passengers. Cut out of heavy duty cardboard it is hinged at the center point for folding and storage and it can also be 'turned' off stage

Music Hall and Variety

This type of show is accepted today as a major part of light entertainment, particularly in clubs and on television.

It is more straightforward to produce than a revue. Self-contained acts requiring the minimum of direction are presented with appropriate link material. It was not always so simple. Political and religious intolerance interfered with the evolution of Music Hall as we know it.

In Britain the 1843 Licensing Act restricted small theaters to music and dancing and those plays which included five musical items in each act, or a musical accompaniment. Production of legitimate drama was forbidden.

By 1850 when Music Hall came into its own, the performers divided into 'legitimate' and 'artistes'. Music Hall became the mainstay of entertainment for the working classes.

Variety was the prime ingredient. Acrobats, magicians and other speciality acts from circus and fairground found their way on to the Music Hall stage. Costume became ever more extravagant and the genre was well established.

For the amateur, this type of production provides a challenge. The separate acts are compiled rather than written, and linking material is kept to a minimum. A Master of Ceremonies positioned between audience and performer provides a physical link, a humorous continuity.

Traditionally, refreshments are available. These can provide an important contribution to a convivial atmosphere and sense of authenticity. There is also a good profit to be made on home made food and a supply of beer!

Royalties are rarely required for material culled from the Victorian era and low production costs means that financial success is more assured.

However, there is a danger of self indulgence. The program must be

varied and balanced. Too many songs and monologues become tedious. Short melodramas, proven magic illusions and character dances all help to build up essential variety. Above all the atmosphere, pace and vitality must be sustained.

By tradition the stage area is the responsibility of the stage manager. The acts and artistes must arrive properly rehearsed and ready to perform, and the design and layout of scenery is organized for them. The combination of stock items, drapes, ground rows, painted rollers and cut cloths will probably be sufficient. If there is a shortage of drapes, hinged, cut profiles will serve. A cat walk built out from the stage with rostra, enclosing all or part of the orchestra, allows the artiste to move out from the stage and into the audience. The Master of Ceremonies can also be positioned just outside the proscenium above eye level so that he or she is in a dominating position and able to control the production and establish that very important contact between performers, orchestra and audience. (If space is at a premium, this 'station' can be built over the top of the piano!)

The overall color scheme should reflect that sumptious quality which epitomized the ornate Music Hall decor.

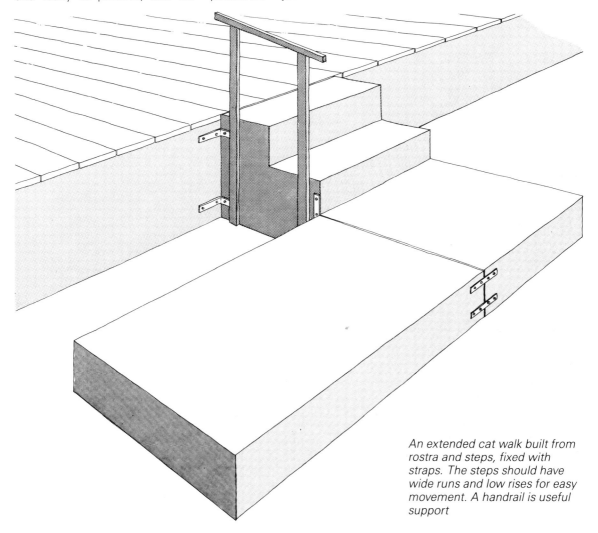

An extended cat walk built from rostra and steps, fixed with straps. The steps should have wide runs and low rises for easy movement. A handrail is useful support

Music Hall and Variety

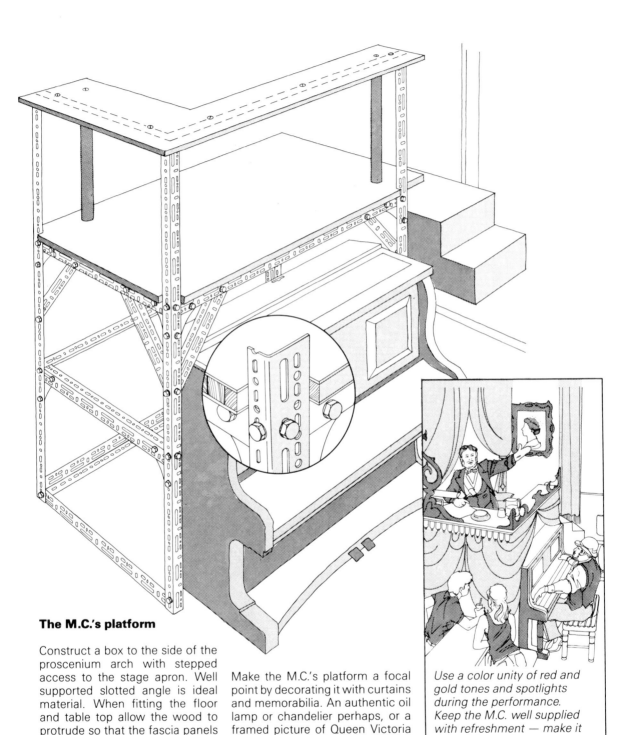

The M.C.'s platform

Construct a box to the side of the proscenium arch with stepped access to the stage apron. Well supported slotted angle is ideal material. When fitting the floor and table top allow the wood to protrude so that the fascia panels can easily be tacked into the board edges at the sides.

Make the M.C.'s platform a focal point by decorating it with curtains and memorabilia. An authentic oil lamp or chandelier perhaps, or a framed picture of Queen Victoria or a famous 19th century local personality or figure-head.

Use a color unity of red and gold tones and spotlights during the performance. Keep the M.C. well supplied with refreshment — make it part of the performance

Properties must also be in keeping. The staff of the wardrobe department need to study the styles of the period. Footwear and waistlines are details which need particularly careful checking. If the audience can be persuaded to arrive in costume, so much the better. There may be a potential source of income from arranging to hire out suitable outfits

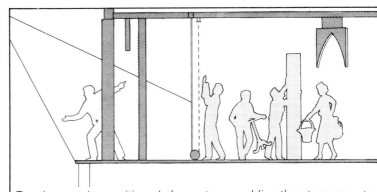

Traveler curtains positioned down stage enabling the stage crew to reset for the next act whilst the preceding act is drawing to a close

Ground rows supported by french braces should be realistically painted — again in pale tones

Dress the auditorium with facsimile posters and handbills. Try to relate them to local industries and traders: you may well encourage those featured to buy advertising space in your program. The arrangement of tables and chairs will obviously reduce the size of the house. Save space by using trestles and benches. These are not only in character but also encourage an intimate team spirit, which, with enthusiastic encouragement by the M.C. and artistes will help to produce the party atmosphere of the old time Music Hall.

If you are using footlights make them more elaborate by adding imitation shields of metal or simply cut them from hardboard

Music Hall and Variety

Disguising the stage crew

The stage crew can be dressed as waiters, with aprons, wing collars, waistcoats etc. In this fashion they can appear on stage and still sustain the historical illusion

Hard masking

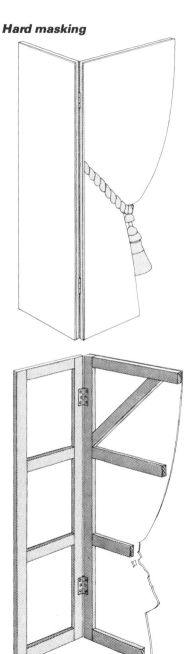

Although soft masking is preferred by the stage crew, hinged or cut profiles can be used if drapes are scarce

Scrolls, cupids and cornucopia need only be cut profiles suspended or tacked over the existing stage front. Gold enamel paint produces a very reasonable fake gilt.

Painting the back-cloth

Soft colors, clean lines and slightly exaggerated perspective provide an unobtrusive background for bright costumes

Musical

Phineas T. Barnum, the unique American showman, possessed a special gift of imagination, impudence and 'sock it to em' razzledazzle. His circus style of presentation, when merged with the popular minstrel shows and combined with the European operetta became the root stock of that most recognizable of American art forms: the Musical.

Glamorous girls and even more glamorous costumes were added in Florenz Zeigfeld's revue of 1907. Twenty years later, *Showboat* with music by Jerome Kern and lyrics by Oscar Hammerstein took the progression one stage further to create a play with music where for the first time the story-line became important.

The remarkable *Oklahoma* produced in 1943, set a new standard. Its verve and vitality fused every aspect of theatrical presentation. Despite a sour critical comment, 'No legs, no laughs, no chance', it took the theater by storm and ran even longer than *Chu Chin Chow*. Dance had become an integral part of the story-line and no longer purely decorative. This innovative approach fundamentally altered the style of the Musical.

From that point onwards, no subject was sacred, no opinion taboo. The Russian pograms in *Fiddler on the Roof*, Nazi oppression in *Cabaret*, the Bible story in *Godspell* have all been portrayed. *Half a sixpence, West Side Story* and *Oliver* are but a few of the flood of musicals produced since World War II.

Although different in content they all combine the exciting elements of theater, and are popular with a public anxious to experience the cheerful energy and vitality of a musical.

A musical is very hard work, very expensive to stage, very tiring to all concerned and, most important, thoroughly enjoyable!

Today's choice of production ranges from the lavishly costumed and richly designed to the functional single setting, from the musically demanding to the simply tuneful.

All musicals demand maximum commitment from the director, designer, cast and support team. Very few are totally beyond the scope of an enthusiastic amateur group — although it is un-economic to run for less than a week in most cases.

Great singing ability is not an essential ingredient. Many stars are renowned not for the quality of

their singing, but for their sincerity and convincing delivery. Do not hesitate to recruit however. Musicals have a way of attracting singers who are later persuaded to take on a wider role in your theater group.

The designer needs to be innovative and resourceful. The average musical involves a larger cast than is usually involved in a straight play and much more is expected of them. The players must have space to dance, sing and speak and this variety of action invariably means a multiplicity of short scenes. *My Fair Lady,* has seventeen, *Oliver,* thirteen and *Camelot,* nineteen.

The absence of sophisticated equipment on most amateur stages means that the dovetailing

of scenery and people requires even greater planning and attention to avoid losing pace and atmosphere.

Examine the synopsis of scenes. Identify the frequency of settings. (Sometimes one can double for another similar scene.) Within the scope of your stage area settle on the key scene on which to base your design. Take into account the number of cast and the activity and movement involved.

In *My Fair Lady,* Professor Higgins' study appears most frequently both in action and dialogue. 'I'm getting married in the morning' is short but very energetic, the Ascot races feature large numbers but little action.

A preliminary model, albeit very basic,is invaluable at this stage (see page 46). While the director's aim is to employ all space profitably, the designer must create that space. Do not hesitate to go beyohd the proscenium arch. Build out, build over, extend the apron, enclose the orchestra. No matter how limited these extensions are, they provide extra points of focus and action while providing some on-stage breathing space for the stage crew. They can be lit separately and also furnished permanently.

Use any fly space. Rollers can have more than one scene painted on them. Traverse curtains require only a ground row to give background to a scene. Trucks, multi-sided flats, hinged units can all play a part in saving time and that valuable space.

The stage is extended on both sides and a convenient space created for the orchestra

Musical

Example: My Fair Lady

Design notes

Victorian London
Covent Garden Market
Wallpaper and curtain material
10 main characters and 20
chorus
Long dresses
Act 1 = 12 musical numbers
Act 11 = 9 combined scenes
— Ascot/Ballroom/Pub
Build truck and Ascot 'tent'
Two-dimensional barrow
2 rollers
21 scenes (5 study, 3 outside
house)

The Music Hall use of a front traverse curtain backing one act, while behind it another more involved setting is being constructed also applies to the Musical. In *My Fair Lady*, the show stopping 'On the street where you live', can be played on the forestage or apron.

This area can be used to denote a street, a shop front, a park, in fact any scene where the set needs only token identification.

With sufficient flying space the arrangement is simple. With restricted space in the stage ceiling a tripped border provides the solution.

Make the upper section of the flown piece in light batten and hardboard and paint the lower section on to canvas, inserting a tripping bar so that the double lift can be employed (See page 97).

Simultaneous flying of the border and drawing of the traverse is another fast and effective scene change technique.

Set changes

MOGG

Traverse curtains allow a scene to be played at the front of the stage, while another setting is being constructed

A successful device used in *My Fair Lady* was a three-sided structure on a truck (see page 80). The 'hollow' side was furnished as part of Professor Higgins' study, with a spiral staircase (made with cardboard and masking tape and definitely not load bearing!) Bookshelves filled with 'two-dimensional' books disguised a door flat. The 'balcony' hid strengthening battens and created an illusion of height. At each side a lightweight window flat was hinged with rich curtain material covering the windows.

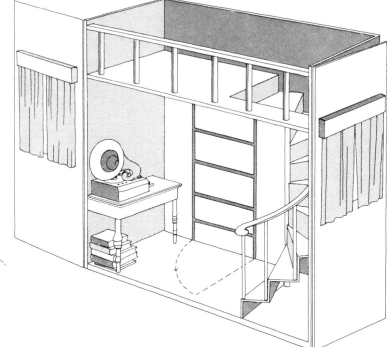

Plan view of Higgins' study, showing hinging arrangement

Plan view of The George, angled against an olio roller

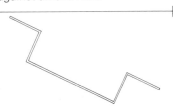

On the reverse side, The George Inn (from which Doolittle emerges) was painted with Victorian lettering and brickwork. Other 'customers' were able to enter from the off stage wings. The truck, when exposing The George, was angled against a roller, concealing most of it and revealing only enough to add perspective and interesting depth to the scene.

Musical

The Embassy ballroom painted
on to a roller with easily moved
trucked pillars in position

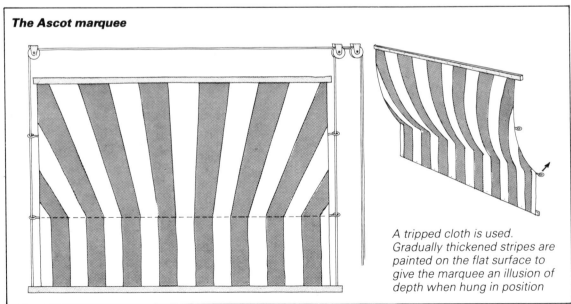

The Ascot marquee

A tripped cloth is used.
Gradually thickened stripes are
painted on the flat surface to
give the marquee an illusion of
depth when hung in position

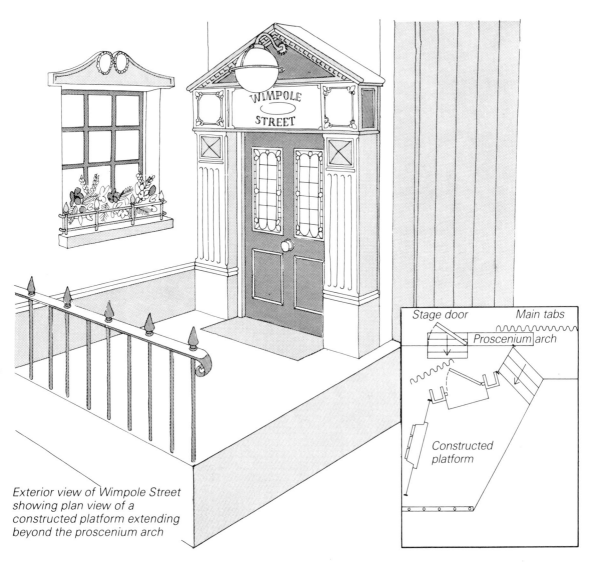

Exterior view of Wimpole Street
showing plan view of a
constructed platform extending
beyond the proscenium arch

Stage door   Main tabs
Proscenium arch
Constructed
platform

To effect a smooth change it is only necessary to divert the eye. One particular sequence in *My Fair Lady* from Act 1 scene 5 will illustrate this. The action moves from Higgins' study to Ascot. From Ascot we go back to Wimpole Street and then into the Embassy ballroom. This complicated procedure was achieved, (with the aid of the small stage extension) thus:

1 Close up and move Higgins' truck up stage

2 Drop tripped Ascot marquee soft cloth

3 Close traveler and bring up light on Wimpole Street

4 Stage extension. Behind traveler, drop Embassy ballroom roller, draw scarlet leg curtains and push on half columns previously used in opening Covent Garden opera scene

5 Dim Wimpole Street. Slowly reveal Embassy ballroom through traveler

Musical

The staging of *Cabaret* requires a totally different approach to *My Fair Lady*. The designer's task is to put across the brittle gaiety of Berlin at the time the Nazi Party was emerging. This is summed up by the decadence of the Kit Kat Club, underlined by the acid humor of the Master of Ceremonies. By making the club setting a permanent one, and designing token scenery to move within it, the atmosphere is encapsulated.

Color is vital to reinforce the feeling of threat. The red, white and black colors of the Nazi flag are very appropriate for the design scheme.

Scenic flow is sustained by removing all curtains and allowing the setting to be changed in full

Plan view

Back wall

Linked trucks

Setting for Kit Kat Club

view of the audience who participate as the Kit Kat Club patrons throughout.

Tables need be no more than token. A section of board I foot (30cm) wide, mounted on a single leg, is sufficient to hold glasses, ashtrays and so on. Individually switched lamps on each table can be switched on and off by the actors.

Small items of scenery, hinged or clipped on, may be added to the truck arrangement illustrated when out of sight of the audience.

Linked trucks

Two trucks are hinged at one corner, providing a selection of sets from one basic unit

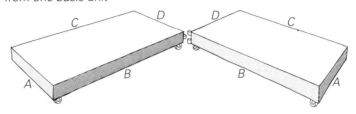

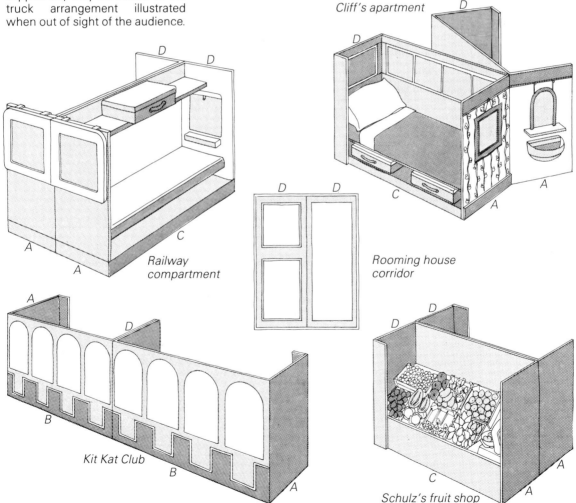

Cliff's apartment

Railway compartment

Rooming house corridor

Kit Kat Club

Schulz's fruit shop

Pantomime

A particularly British tradition, the pantomime makes its annual appearance at Christmas as entertainment for the whole family. Over the years it has become a mixture of the performing arts and a vehicle for the leading entertainers of the day. A hotchpotch of comedy, dance, romance and slapstick, its roots lie in the improvised comedy of the 16th century: the Italian *commedia dell' arte*. A group of professional actors performed well-established storylines but improvised the dialogue. This spontaneity was helped by characters whose particular costume immediately identified them to the audience.

The diamond patchwork and broad brimmed hat was the uniform of Harlequin, and Colombine's costume was a multicolored dress and half mask.

Music Hall introduced sumptuous costume, broad comedy and spectacular effects into the proceedings. The thread of the plot was sustained but frequently interrupted by variety turns and popular songs.

Today, the male hero is traditionally played by a leggy actress and the part of the Dame by the chief comedian dressed as a woman in ridiculous costume. Good is personified by the Good Fairy or Fairy Godmother and Evil by the Demon King or the Wicked Witch.

The whole production must be larger than life and twice as colorful. Transformation is all part of the entertainment.

Although the pantomime itself is unsophisticated, the scenery and moving parts will require considerable work. To make the whole project worth while, the run must extend to at least a week. This will add greatly to the contribution asked of the stage crew and the stamina demanded of the cast.

In all pantomimes, smooth running changes of scene are all important. At times these need to appear 'before your very eyes' and the pace of the production depends on the versatility, color and mobility of the scenery units. Placing a roller or a traverse curtain well down stage does provide some time for 'behind the scenes' activity.

A magic carpet chase

No pantomime should be without a 'chase'. It diverts the eye and its timing can be adjusted if necessary to allow more time to effect the next complicated change.

The physical dimensions of your stage will probably prevent actual continuous movement. In the high days of the Victorian theater, the effect was achieved by a continuous roller mounted horizontally. This unit is uneconomical for amateur productions. An alternative is physically to carry the scenery past the stationary pursuers.

The illustration sets the scene for 'Arabia' but it could well be the Enchanted Forest or Never Never Land. Behind a tripped border, stage hands carry the cut out profiles of palm trees, temples and palaces.

The scene takes on comic proportions when the pursuers,

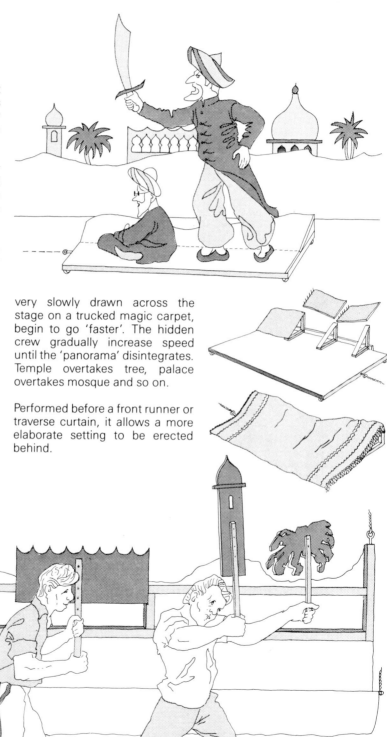

very slowly drawn across the stage on a trucked magic carpet, begin to go 'faster'. The hidden crew gradually increase speed until the 'panorama' disintegrates. Temple overtakes tree, palace overtakes mosque and so on.

Performed before a front runner or traverse curtain, it allows a more elaborate setting to be erected behind.

Pantomime

In all pantomimes awkward scene changes occur — from dingy kitchen to sumptous ballroom. How will Cinderella's coach appear and then move off stage carrying her to the ball? Jack's beanstalk must grow and then be climbed. Use the devices described here and in previous chapters to manipulate scenery.

Gauzes, painted rollers and back-cloths, ground rows and trucks must all be made to dovetail into a critical timescale.

A symmetrical coach profile is used to allow Cinderella to drive off and then arrive at the ball.

The truck containing the coach is laid down on stage at the beginning of the scene. At the moment of flash and smoke, the cut profile is lifted into position. The hinged braces will keep it upright.

A stage hand standing behind the coach can hold the coachman in position. Two identical coachmen, (one reversed) can 'drive' away the coach in either direction. There is traditionally a curtain at the end of this scene to enable Cinderella to 'enter' the coach and be driven off stage by a tow rope.

Cinderella's coach

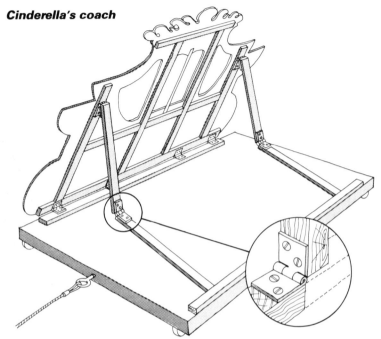

The coach is hinged to a truck which is then drawn across stage by a cable

Reverse side of coachman showing 'handle' for stage crew

Two coachmen are required — one for moving off stage right to the ball, one for returning from stage right

Interior unit for Cinderella

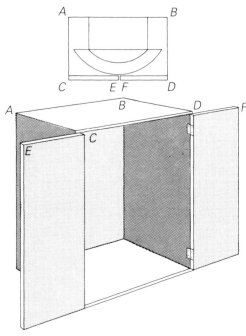

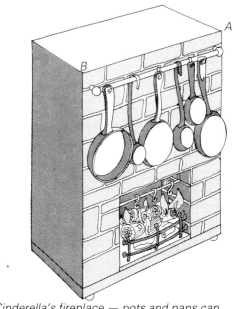

Cinderella's fireplace — pots and pans can be painted on

The ugly sisters' window is not transparent. 'Ugly' curtains are added to the top edge of the hinged windows

The Prince's throne is richly furnished and lit from behind curtains. The seat is the top of the fireplace

Pantomime

Jack's beanstalk

A garden is painted boldly on to a ground row. The ground row disguises the beanstalk storage box. Beanstalk and leaves are glued or painted on to gauze. Avoid loose edges which can cause tangling. Hoist the beanstalk using a black cable

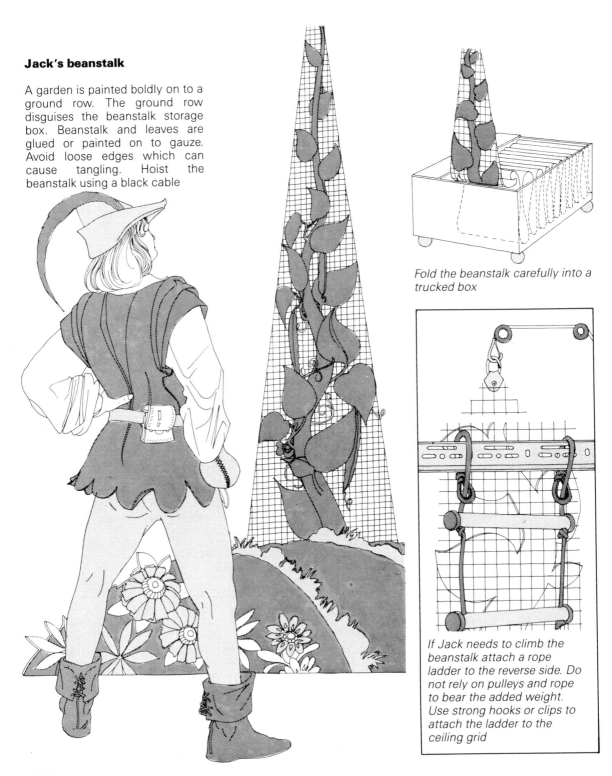

Fold the beanstalk carefully into a trucked box

If Jack needs to climb the beanstalk attach a rope ladder to the reverse side. Do not rely on pulleys and rope to bear the added weight. Use strong hooks or clips to attach the ladder to the ceiling grid

Space saving bed

Build a light wooden framework and add hardboard to the top section. Paint on pillows and suitable decoration. Cover the bed bottom with hardboard and paint 'bedclothes' on to the bedboard.

The bed is constructed from these three sections. A batten and hook link the 'headboard' to the foot of the bed. The hinges allow the construction to fold flat for easy storage

Drama for young children

Young people love dressing up in costume. Their powers of imagination and uncomplicated emotions enable them to 'believe' with enthusiasm. This ability is an important part of their overall development and is the very stuff of acting. Performing simple plays is rewarding for the young actors, their teachers and parents.

The traditional Christmas story illustrates the point perfectly. Dressed in robes, cloaks, wings and crowns, the children handle props convincingly and become even more involved in the story than the audience. The story can be portrayed with mime and commentary or as an entirely choral piece. Dramatizing fairy stories and poems in the same way, will bring them to life.

Scenery plays a small but not unimportant part in productions of this nature, but the designer must bear in mind that visibility is all important. An arena or in the round setting in the school hall or gymnasium is ideal. It helps everyone to see and provides ample space for movement.

Decoration should be in prime bright colors with plenty of shine and sparkle. Aluminum foil or silver dust sprinkled on to a glued surface is effective. Patterned decor can be prepared in class beforehand.

Beware of excessive lighting. It can prove uncomfortable and disconcerting to a young cast.

Rostra and ground rows

All stage units must be miniaturized. Rostra must be at a low level, of no more than 6 inches (15cm). Small legs cannot negotiate several levels, especially when encumbered with unfamiliar clothes. Make steps wide and low with a long run and a short rise. Place handrails in position at the highest point.

If ground rows are necessary build support on to the front as well as the back to make them sturdy and safe. The unplanned collapse of a mountain would cause dismay and confusion.

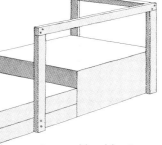

Low rostrum with wide steps, a short rise and a firm handrail

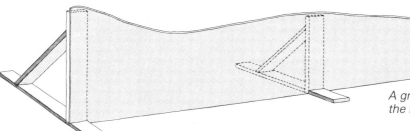

A ground row supported at both the front and back for stability

Back-cloths

Back-cloths need be no larger than bed sheets. Soak them in size first and apply a coat of white emulsion when they are dry. This provides a good surface on which to paint with tempera or powder colors. Mix a little wallpaper paste with the paint to give it more body and prevent dusting when dry. Thread a pole, bamboo or doweling, at the top and bottom of the cloth to produce an even, smooth surface on which to paint. High jump supports will keep the back-cloth in place.

A back-cloth is supported with high jump props borrowed from the sports department

Temporary scenery

Make all scenery lightweight. Stiff cardboard or paper glued or stapled to a light timber frame of 1½ x ½ inch (38 x 12mm) batten will suffice, the structure does not have to be permanent. Reinforce it with corner triangles of plywood

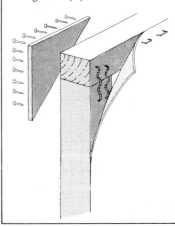

Drama for juniors

As children grow physically and mentally, so their potential for drama increases. Drama lessons help to develop poise and confidence through speech, movement and improvisation and the technical aspects of production can also prove fascinating.

From the age of nine upwards children are able to make a much more positive contribution to a production. They enjoy applying their own make up and prop making is an ideal way for them to develop their practical and artistic skills in a fun way.

More ambitious plays can be performed because at this age children are very keen to memorize lines (often to the extent that they will learn everyone else's too!) They realise that each role is part of a greater whole, and respond accordingly. Younger children tend to perform set pieces in isolation.

Juniors should be encouraged to think about and give some individuality to the characters they portray. Twenty villains (the robber band in The Snow Queen for example) should not appear identically dressed and all gruffly spoken! (Remember, however, that young voices do not carry very well, and keep out of doors productions very visual.)

Being on a stage before an audience is a real discipline, and it is the responsibility of the adult in control to provide the best possible setting in which the children can learn the skills and feel a real sense of achievement. This is not always easy. Only a minority of schools boast a real stage. Too often the main hall must be multipurpose.

Build a temporary construction of units or rostra. Lightweight stage blocks are versatile and load bearing, and fixed firmly together make an adequate stage. They can also serve as castles or ships in an arena or outdoor presentation.

Appropriately made step units are essential. They must fit well together to avoid annoying squeaks and groans. The floor must be absolutely level to avoid accidents. Cover the surface with hardboard sheets well scarified to remove the polished surface.

Folding rostra, as illustrated on page 70, although expensive to make, are quickly erected and dismantled. Their construction is one area where the talents of the P.T.A. may well be exploited.

With a basic stage, children can begin to learn the elements of stage craft: entrances, exits, grouping and timing. Lighting the stage requires more funds (although your local dramatic society may exchange lighting equipment for the loan of your child actors!) You will need only the most basic lamps for front and side lighting to create a 'magic' atmosphere.

School productions necessarily involve large numbers which may cause 'flow' problems. Here the simple proscenium becomes inadequate. Extend the apron to make a thrust stage. The traverse curtains will allow new scenes to be set behind this 'runner'. Use entrances through the audience and from side doors so that the whole hall becomes one big

theater. The audience will enter into the spirit of the performance, but the children will not lose their fantasy world.

Involve the children in planning and organizing. This is how the stage managers and designers of the future are created. Take time to arrange the backstage storage area. Allocate particular places for particular pieces and instruct your youthful assistant stage managers in the importance of careful and convenient storage. Give each of them a list of tasks and practise the change sequence both before and during rehearsals.

Drama for juniors

A thrust stage

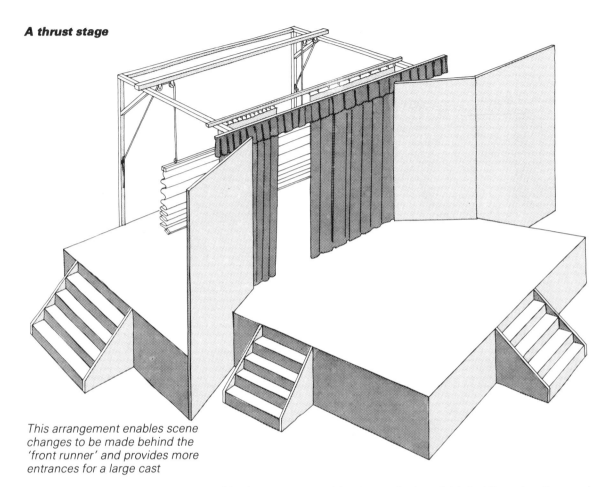

This arrangement enables scene changes to be made behind the 'front runner' and provides more entrances for a large cast

The numbers involved require extra space and 'collection' areas backstage. Wide steps are essential to allow easy access. The absence of furniture on stage means that back-cloths provide a rapid change of scene for both cast and audience. They may have to be changed swiftly. Make them of light material with a batten bearing several hooks. These can be attached to a lowered batten with eyelets and pulled back into position while the other back-cloth is moved off stage. Light cotton sheets glued together are quite adequate. They should be sized, stretched flat and hung on a thin batten to provide a good surface. Mix school tempera or poster color with paste or size to prevent 'dusting' but do not make it so thick that it cracks after rough handling. Get the children to fill in the outlines of the design.

A simple back-cloth hoist

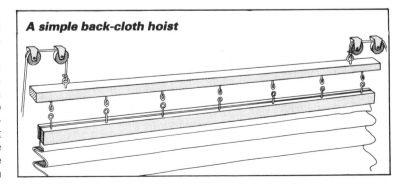

All scenery must be lightweight and easily moved. Make it serve as many purposes as possible. A cupboard which reverses to show an oven, a 'wall' on a trucked unit showing an interior set on one side and an exterior on the other.

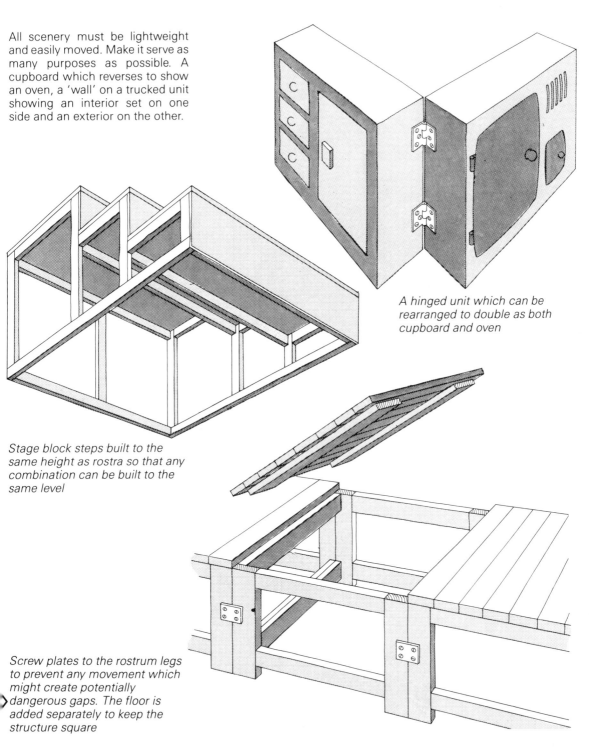

A hinged unit which can be rearranged to double as both cupboard and oven

Stage block steps built to the same height as rostra so that any combination can be built to the same level

Screw plates to the rostrum legs to prevent any movement which might create potentially dangerous gaps. The floor is added separately to keep the structure square

Drama for teenagers

Teenagers are usually gregarious, energetic and have few inhibitions. Their awareness of character, costume and make up is very much a part of their everyday experience. Physically they are adult, but with a refreshingly open minded approach to life that their parents may have lost. The school study curriculum will encourage discussion, exploration and understanding of the text of a play and the teenager will approach stage problems with imagination and innovation.

This age group is also very demanding. They seek excellence and excitement. A teaching commitment is essential and any program must be a busy one to sustain enthusiasm.

In schools, workshops and specialist departments for music, art, design and woodwork, happily take the place of those sections aimed for in an adult theater group, but they contain a wider opportunity for adventure and participation. A particular theater problem can give a valid and practical point to pure theory in the syllabus. Flat or rostrum construction may become a technical exercise while scene painting and costume design may legitimately be considered as part of a series of lessons.

The theater workshop provides the opportunity for drama in all forms. Unscripted activity, practising movement, mime, and voice production are all relevant. Each aspect is polished and improved but in a loose and enjoyable atmosphere where the group works together and shares ideas. School facilities may be available or an adult theater group may help with equipment.

This very productive but relatively unstructured development lends itself more readily to an arena, thrust, or in the round mode of presentation. The energy of young people is best exploited on these wider stage shapes. The disciplines of the prosenium stage may be introduced at a later point in the workshop program.

The open approach is an excellent opportunity for experimentation. Simplistic settings made with adaptable units making use of different levels, give a more uncluttered stage area and provide specific performing areas and a variety of entrances.

Where drama is part of a school's curriculum, the learning process is structured. After extensive exploration of individual acting skills, the young people learn how to relate to the acting space. The effects achieved by grouping and blocking are aided by the most basic of stage units. Rostra of different shapes and sizes, simple benches and stools, ramps and steps, all provide an alternative to a flat surface.

They can be placed in a variety of positions to create arena or in the round acting areas as well as on the traditional stage level.

When making them, remember they must be robust enough to support the sometimes exuberant but not always lightfooted performers. Add a strip of rubber to the bottom edges to act as a brake when using the units on a polished floor.

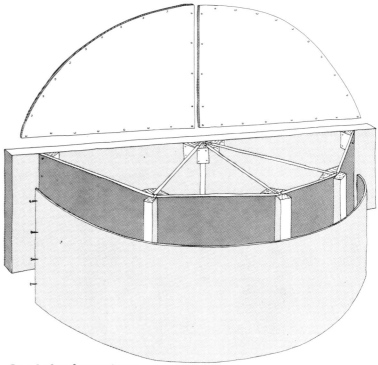

Semi-circular rostrum

To build a semi-circular shape, support curved panels of hardboard with pieces of timber. Screw the top sections down and reinforce with angled joints and timber blocks. Screw and glue the main structure together

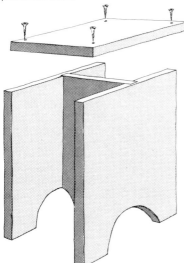

A simple stool constructed from 9 x l inch (228 x 25mm) softwood. Particle board is a cheaper alternative but requires painting

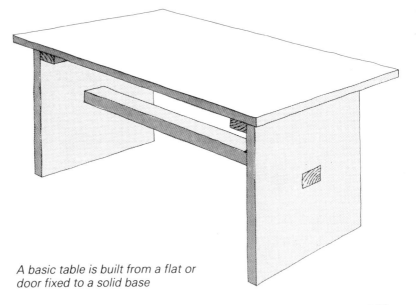

A basic table is built from a flat or door fixed to a solid base

Drama for teenagers

Constructing a stairway

The 'run' is greater than the 'rise'.
To lift to 3 feet (90cm) the run
total will be 4 feet (120cm) at an
angle of 40°. Use 10 x 1 inch
(254 x 25mm) for stair sides and
stair treads. Reinforce
horizontally with timber blocks
and strengthen vertically with
screws and glue. Insert a metal
rod with threaded ends and bend
the nut to prevent the stairway
from coming apart. Use angled
brackets to secure the top and
bottom

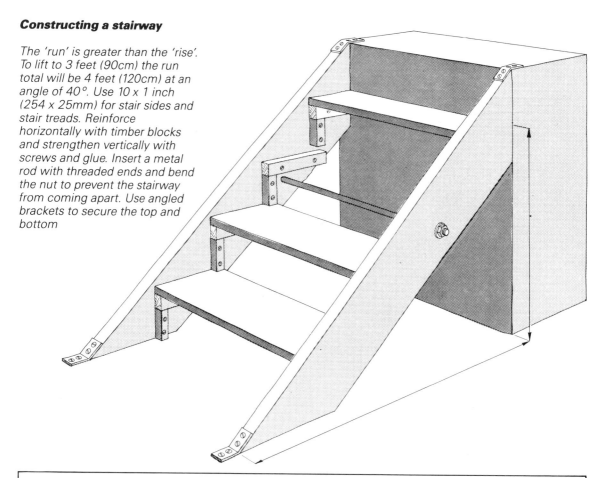

Wide steps

For wider, lower steps use a
series of step-high rostra blocks
of progressively wider
dimensions. The lift or rise
however, should be constant at
between 6 and 9 inches
(15 and 23cm) and the run must
always be longer than the rise

Lengths of 7 inches and 1 inch
(177mm and 25mm) wood are
glued and screwed together.
Reinforce the corners and, if
over 5 feet (1½m) long, insert a
slotted section into the center

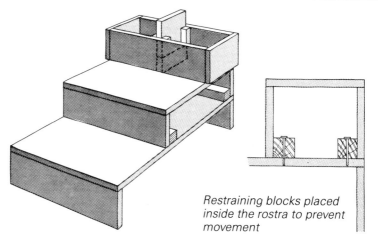

Restraining blocks placed
inside the rostra to prevent
movement

Agility and energy are two teenage attributes. Any stage construction must be load bearing.

Link rostra steps, ramps, and so on together with angle brackets and, if permitted, screw brake battens into the stage floor. Assembling the rostra units on a stage cloth is an alternative.

If the script demands fast entry from up stage, position the brake batten on the downstage edge.

Alternative steps

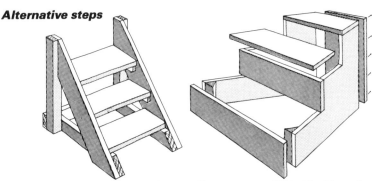

These are a similar construction to the stairway except smaller and more versatile

Cut a step profile in blockboard, reinforce the corners and then add the steps

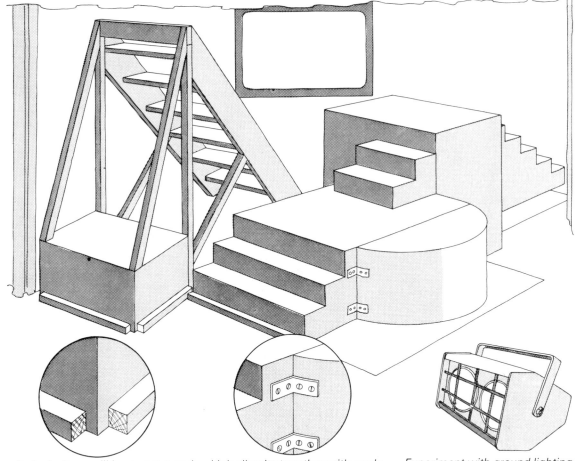

Brake battens will keep rostra and steps in position

Link all units together with angle brackets

Experiment with ground lighting but protect power cables

Festival and competitive drama

There is a danger that by maintaining an insular attitude to theater, choosing familiar plays and presenting them to the same audience with stale predictable staging, you will fail to stimulate the public, and lose support.

An effective counter to this complacency lies with the well established custom of competitive or festival drama. These competitions vary in practice but the principles remain the same. Plays are judged by an outsider, a professional adjudicator with wide experience who applies objective standards to each competing production.

A group will learn much about alternative methods of presentation, play selection and scene design, and its internal organization will be tested against others. By watching other societies perform, your group cannot fail to pick up new ideas and inspiration.

The One Act Festival illustrates the system well. The event is held at a single playhouse. Each company performs on the same stage to a strict time schedule before the resident adjudicator.

At the end of the festival the adjudicator makes a decision, chooses the winners and presents the awards for the best play, actor, actress, set designer, stage manager and so on. This is the real point of the competition and the objective criticisms put those 'you were wonderful' comments in true perspective.

The marks cover all aspects of a production. They vary in value but cumulatively influence the final decisions.

Presentation involves scene design, lighting, wardrobe, make up and all aspects of stage management. Production relates to the interpretation of the script, the cast's awareness and understanding of the director's view and their skill in performance.

Local sponsorship by newspapers and television has not only increased the competitive edge by widening the catchment area but has also encouraged new writers of the one act play. The winning of these regional 'oscars' carries considerable kudos for actor and company alike. All departments of the group are on show. They can all share success, but more importantly, they can all learn from the detailed adjudication.

Briefings enable directors and stage managers to examine and explore the host theater, to make the most of its shape and its facilities and to cope with its disadvantages.

The lighting possibilities, the difficulties of access, available wing space and flying capability will certainly influence the design and general presentation.

Time restrictions both in setting up and striking will further complicate the design concept and time and space savers may well be the only effective solution. Easily constructed and easily moved units are ideal. Trucks, split hinges, and so on should all be exploited. Lightweight materials, the more versatile the better, may be used to advantage. You are aiming for a temporary set that works, not a lasting effect.

Moving scenery from the home base presents problems. Trailers, vans and roof racks attached to members' cars must be organized and coordinated. Accurate directions and a trouble-free route will enable all parts of the set to arrive in good time and in fit condition.

Festival and competitive drama

A trucked two scene unit

In a one act but two-scened play
'Pageant faded', it may be
necessary to change from palace
to hovel. Mount split-hinged flats
on to a truck. Screw timber
battens to the truck surface
against which the flat bottoms are
attached by hooks or angle
brackets. The hovel table and shelf
are also split-hinged and
supported by french braces.

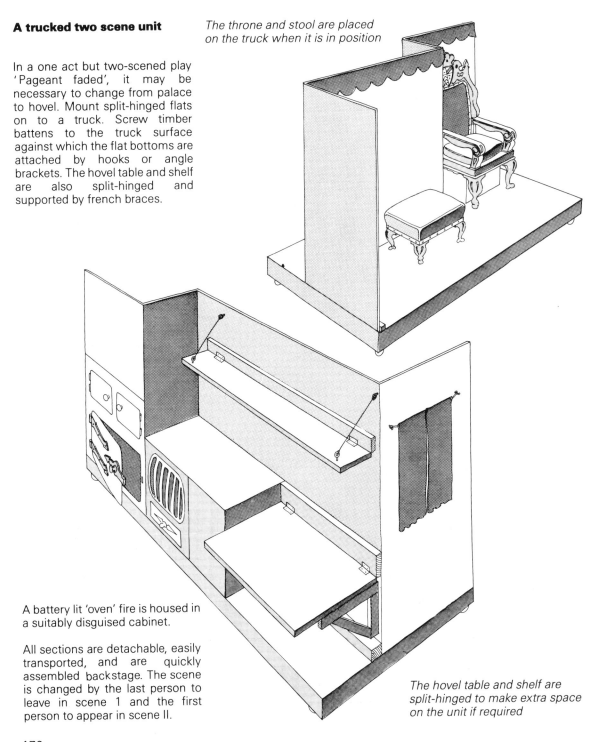

*The throne and stool are placed
on the truck when it is in position*

A battery lit 'oven' fire is housed in
a suitably disguised cabinet.

All sections are detachable, easily
transported, and are quickly
assembled backstage. The scene
is changed by the last person to
leave in scene 1 and the first
person to appear in scene II.

*The hovel table and shelf are
split-hinged to make extra space
on the unit if required*

Hinged scenery units

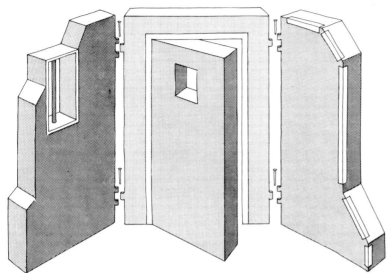

A token set and door which is very lightweight and easily and quickly put together. The angle of the 'wing' flats will add stability and counter the door movement. To give the impression of thickness, glue and nail blocks to the edge of the main 'wall'

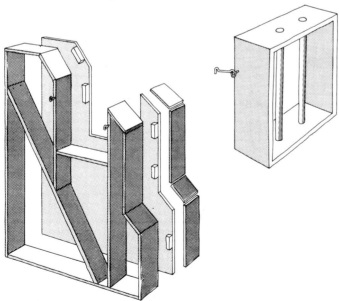

Add 'width' sections of hardboard. Seal edges with masking tape before painting. Add 'thickness' to the door and spyhole. Build a window separately to fit inside the wing. Secure by hook and eye to the wing flat

Suspended scenic units

With a curtain set, token scenery is sufficient to create the setting

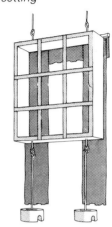

Screw eyelets into the top and bottom of the window frame. Clip base cables on to stage weights. Attach top cables to a batten. Paint cables matte black

Tall units, doors and french windows all require a similar tension by weight and cable into the flies. There is no need to install a working door

Have set will travel

Taking theater into the community gives the group an ideal opportunity to show its wares — to display its own particular merchandise to a potential audience. If the group has a full blown 'in-house' production scheduled soon afterwards it is also an excellent time to distribute publicity material.

Festivals, fêtes and historical anniversaries are all suitable venues. A ready-made play may be appropriate or you may need to invent a special script.

Taking a play out of the theater requires a fresh approach to set construction. Scale is reduced, and the set needs to be versatile and portable. Two and three fold flats, folding rostra, simple curtain tracks and wall hangings are the key items for a successful one-night stand.

Size and shape will be governed by the dimensions and head room of the temporary stage and the means of transportation.

For a portable flat to be manageable, its dimensions should not exceed 8 x 3 feet (243 x 90cm). If sack cloth is used as the covering material, size and paint this with emulsion paints. The consistency of the paint helps fill the surface weave and presents a smoother surface. Audiences in 'ad hoc' situations are usually seated closer to the scenery, so careful and more detailed designs are required than for a normal stage setting. For hangings, collage is most suitable, with paint as a decorating medium.

Use the 'stage' floor wherever possible to compliment the basic setting. Transfer your sketch on to the floor cloth by the squared scale method (see page 122). Mark the position of flats, props and furniture with tape. Don't spend time decorating areas which are permanently masked; concentrate on those visible to the audience. Make the design bold and uncomplicated.

Unusual situations must be accommodated by the designer and existing openings also incorporated into his design. Respect the fabric of your temporary stage. Don't knock nails into ancient timbers or drill into venerated stonework. Such places as churches or inn yards already provide a natural setting. Any imported scenery must blend

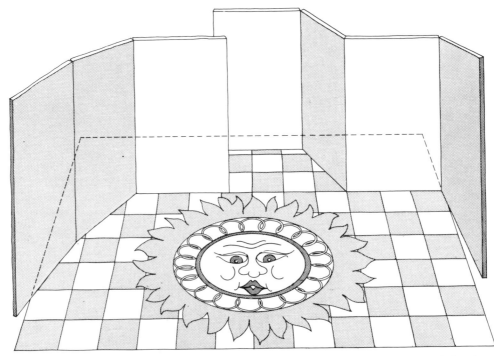

Make the floor cloth design colorful, combined with hinged flats it will make a good basis for the set

172

in and be free standing. It will probably need anchoring with stage weights.

Organizing the fit-up will require tight coordination from all departments. The designer must visit the site along with the director and stage manager to discover lighting requirements, maximum dimensions, access and changing facilities. Correctly shaped transport for scenery, costume and lights must then be laid on in good time and a timetable established.

Striking the set requires the same degree of control and planning to avoid damage by careless helpers, and correct storage back at base must be organized. It is hectic, it is demanding, but it is fun!

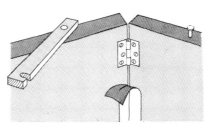

A restraining brace holds unit firm and swings back so that the flats 'fold' neatly

A quickly dismantled pin hinge, secure the pin to the flat with a length of string

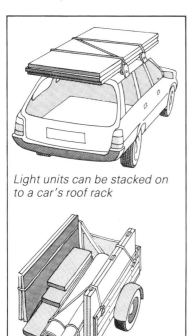

Light units can be stacked on to a car's roof rack

Heavier items may be placed on a trailer and towed

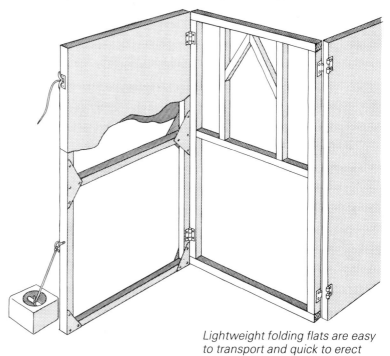

Lightweight folding flats are easy to transport and quick to erect

Banners

A double-faced banner or tapestry assembled on canvas from a collage of materials is very impressive

Different plays in different ways

Some lavish musicals were written with large casts and huge professional stages in mind and the demands of this type of staging will usually be beyond the scope of a local society.

Do not despair! If you can gain wholehearted commitment from all departments of your amateur group this enthusiasm will open the door to a wide variety of shows, plays and 'theatrical happenings'.

Unlike musical or operatic societies, your group does not need to major on a single annual production. Comedy, farce, thriller and revue can all feature in one year's program of entertainment.

The number of performances of any particular play is limited for several reasons. The size of the 'house', other societies' use of the 'theater' facilities and the stamina of the cast, some of whom may have full-time jobs and heavy family commitments, are all contributing factors. Short runs unfortunately mean that, all too frequently, it is the scenery design and construction which suffers from shortage of time.

The designer's task begins as soon as the current production is under way. You must ignore the existing setting on stage and, with the aid of models, plans and a vivid imagination, set about the design process for the following production. Make the most of the existing stage but do not be inhibited by it. Work with the director to put across a unique interpretation.

Just as different directors see the same play in different ways so the designer must introduce a variety of style and approach into his work to avoid becoming stale. If the audience is charmed, amused or intrigued by the set, the play as a whole will give much more satisfaction.

Try something new; look at staging problems afresh, but always bear in mind that 'the play's the thing' and after the director, the audience will give the final verdict by, hopefully, filling those seats more frequently.

Under Milkwood

This is certainly a very different play. Dylan Thomas wrote it originally for radio but it has subsequently been transposed most successfully to the stage. It is an ingenious piece of poetic drama, full of good humor and intriguing characters. The audience is invited to look into the hopes, fears, dreams and realities of the inhabitants of a small Welsh village during one day and night. The pace of the play is dictated by the quick-fire cameo nature of the script. Because it is essentially a play for voices, the designer has enormous freedom and scope. The setting can be realistic, stylized, or only partly representational. Because the cast is large, access from different parts of the stage needs to be straightforward and uncluttered. Numerous entrances should be provided and a variety of levels is essential to sustain interest and involvement.

There are two narrators who introduce characters and maintain continuity, but at no time must they distract the eye from the action.

Thrust/extended apron

Build a scaffold structure across the proscenium 6 feet 6 inches (198cm) high. Access is by one onstage staircase with 8 or 9 steps, and by two offstage stairways.

For stability and extra security, extend the vertical section of the scaffold to support a handrail. Use curtains at ground level to allow easy entrances.

Build a separate rostra for Captain Cat's house down stage left. The upper level house profiles double as bedheads. Paint these simply,

the cast will appear over them, the front row sitting, the second row standing. Support the ground rows by french brace (see page 59), angled at 85° to exaggerate the angle of vision.

The focus is changed by lighting, which moves from character to character and area to area, as the script dictates.

Token decoration of the stage level compartments is sufficient, with a variety of tables and chairs. The bar can also serve as a shop cupboard by simple reversing.

By leaving the top of the cyclorama in view, simple ground rows or projected slides can be lit or silhouetted.

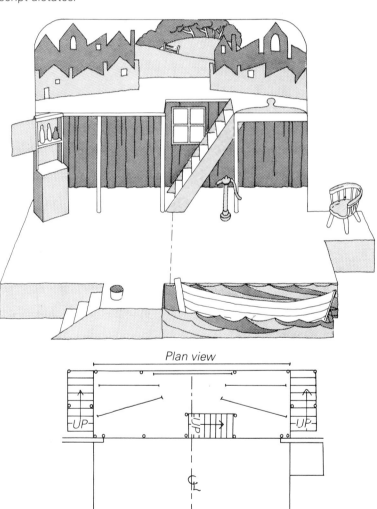

Plan view

The actors take their places behind house profiles, these are made from hardboard, supported by french braces and angled at 85° so that they lean backwards. The audience gets the impression of 'looking up the hill' as a result

The higher level ground rows only need to be half constructed as the actors will stand behind them. This will also save weight

A two-dimensional boat for No-good Billy

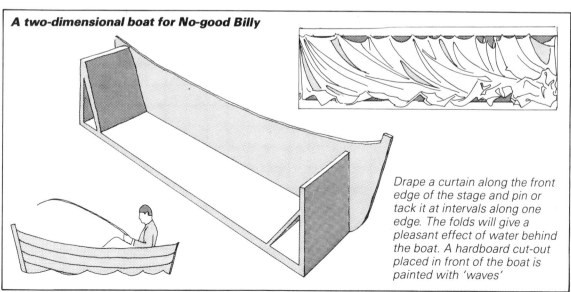

Drape a curtain along the front edge of the stage and pin or tack it at intervals along one edge. The folds will give a pleasant effect of water behind the boat. A hardboard cut-out placed in front of the boat is painted with 'waves'

Under Milkwood

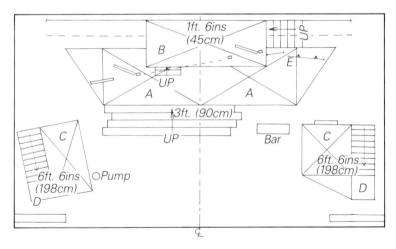

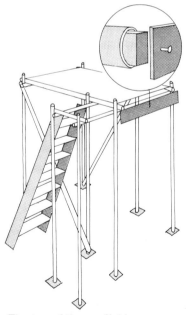

The top of the scaffold construction is 6 x 8 feet (182 x 243cm). Place a timber 'plug' into the scaffold pole and nail on a hardboard pelmet

A The major rostra construction is 3 feet (90cm) high

B The rearmost rostra is 18 inches (45cm) high

C The scaffold construction allows 6 feet 6 inches (198cm) headroom

D Stairway access is stage right, ladder access is stage left

E Ground rows — consist of three profiles and a leaf border

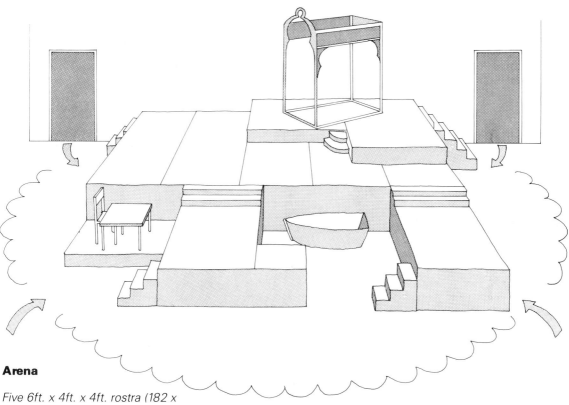

Arena

Five 6ft. x 4ft. x 4ft. rostra (182 x 120 x 120cm)

Four 6ft. x 3ft. x 3ft. rostra (182 x 90 x 90cm)

One 8ft. x 6ft. x 1ft. rostra (243 x 182 x 30cm)

Because this setting will remain throughout the play, you can afford to put time, effort and imagination into building an impressive set. Many different levels and varied forms of access will all help to direct the audience's attention from one character to another.

The stage will require a focal point, preferably at a high level. A simply made Shop/chapel, as illustrated, will suffice. Lighting is the key. Pre-arranged areas can be lit, leaving the rest in shadow.

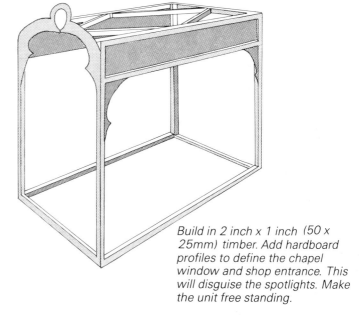

Build in 2 inch x 1 inch (50 x 25mm) timber. Add hardboard profiles to define the chapel window and shop entrance. This will disguise the spotlights. Make the unit free standing.

The Crucible

Written by the American dramatist, Arthur Miller, this play is based on the witch trials of the 17th century, but at the same time it is a very thinly veiled attack on Senator Joe McCarthy's famous witchhunt against communists in the United States.

Proscenium arch set

To mount a four act play on a restricting proscenium arched stage, particularly when the properties are bulky, creates problems. A very necessary point of this play's action is the steady increase of hysteria which builds up until the dramatic final scene. Tension may well be lost if too much time is taken between acts on complicated scene changes. In these circumstances it may be wise to establish a basic, somewhat anonymous, box setting, against which the furniture and, in particular, the cast, may move smoothly in their cloaks and bulky gowns.

By adding casters to most of the furniture units you will be able to change scenery quickly. Simple adjustments to the traverse curtains will both extend and curtail the basic set dimensions. Controlled lighting will also obscure parts of a plain set and concentrate the attention on the main acting areas.

If it speeds up the overall pace, have the stage crew suitably costumed to move the furniture units in full view of the audience.

The architecture of the period was plain and generally at a low level. No flying of units is necessary, but the lighting team will need to work above head height backstage. Allow for this activity in the wings.

The basic set construction

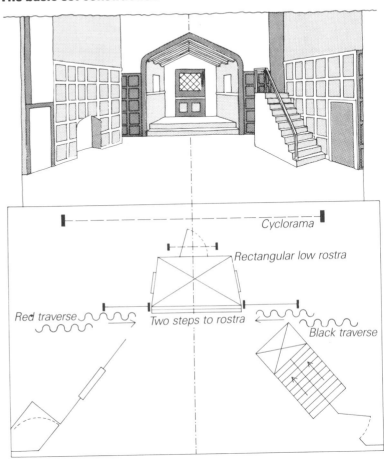

Cyclorama

Rectangular low rostra

Red traverse

Two steps to rostra

Black traverse

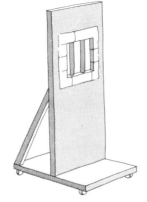

Trucked cell window flat

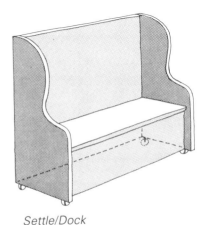

Settle/Dock

The scene changes

Bedroom

Bedroom to living room

1 Move stair truck to wall
2 Move out bed. Lift one flap to reveal table
3 Remove window/door filler
4 Push settle to fireside
5 Move dressers on stage
6 Light fireplace area
7 Light cyclorama

Living room to courtroom

1 Close red traverse
2 Reverse dresser to reveal bookcase
3 Reverse settle to act as dock
4 Open both sides of table
5 Push steps off stage
6 Spotlight dock and magistrate's bench

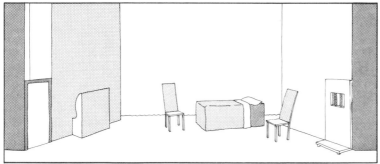

Courtroom to cell

1 Close black traverse
2 Close up table and dress as bed
3 Leave settle covering fireplace
4 Lower lighting to highlight stage left door
5 Light high up stage left

The Crucible

Curtain set

The advantage of a curtain set lies in its simplicity. All moods are easily established by lighting. The settings are identified by furniture only. The actors become the center of focus because there is nothing to distract attention away from them.

If period furniture is unobtainable, contemporary pieces can easily be adapted by the addition of cut profiles and careful painting. In the final cell scene it heightens the dramatic tension and concentrates the attention if the main tabs are drawn part way. Check sight-lines to fix the most suitable drawing point. Use a stage level

and suspended floodlight on the sky-cloth. Gelatines may be changed behind the traverse.

Do not overdecorate the set. The action takes place at the time when the Puritans considered the elaborate carving of the Elizabethan period to be the work of the devil!

Act One   Bedroom

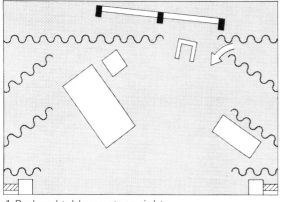

1 Bed and table up stage right
2 Chair off center up stage left
3 Chest or settle down stage left
4 Back traverse closed to reveal window stage left

Act Two   Living room

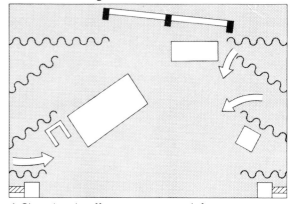

1 Chest/settle off center up stage left
2 Bed removed, table from center to down stage right
3 Chair down stage right
4 Small table down stage left
5 Both windows revealed

Act Three   Meeting House

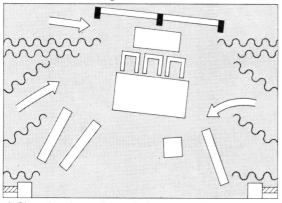

1 Chest/settle against window up stage center
2 Table and chairs up stage center
3 Benches down stage right and down stage left
4 Pull red traverse into center

Act Four   Cell

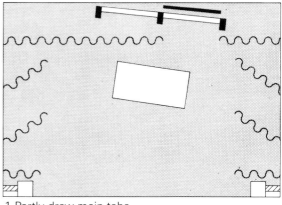

1 Partly draw main tabs
2 Draw black traverse to reveal window
3 Place window filler with bars into stage left window
4 Reset bed down stage center stage left

Arena set

The key here is to establish levels. Directional lighting from above will isolate particular areas but those areas not lit should not intrude into the audience's vision. By placing the higher levels up stage the eye is drawn up and over the thrust whilst the thrust area itself is ignored. Little or no scene changing is required, because particular areas have been established by lighting and physical positioning. Numerous entrances on stage and from the auditorium further involve and stimulate the audience.

Although the rostra need not be decorated with more than a textured surface, props should be made to look as authentic as possible, because of their close proximity to the audience. Make use of the floor area; rush matting is appropriate to this play. Take care to anchor the highest rostra.

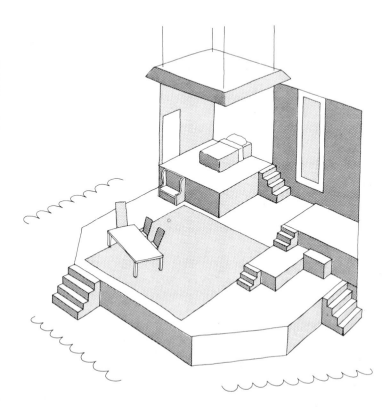

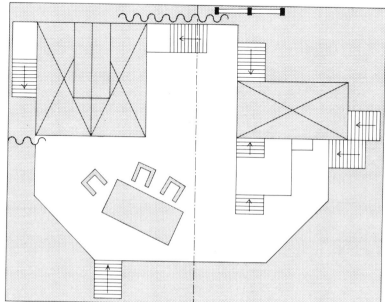

Furniture
One lightweight bed
One small table
One chest
One settle
One refectory table
Two chairs, stools, rush matting

Rostra
Three 8ft. long x 4ft. high x 4ft. wide (243 x 120 x 120cm)
Two 4ft. x 4ft. x 2ft. (120 x 120 x 60cm)

Flats
Plain 4ft. x 3ft. (120 x 90cm)
Window 1ft. x 4ft. (30 x 120cm)
Long window flat

Steps
4 x 4ft. (120cm) rise
2 x 2ft. (60cm) rise
2 x arena steps

Oh what a lovely war

Oh What A Lovely War is a chronicle in song and documents of the 1914-18 period. It was written by Charles Chilton and members of the Theatre Workshop cast and first presented by Theatre Workshop at the Theatre Royal in London's East End in 1963.

Joan Littlewood, the director and moving spirit behind Theatre Workshop aimed to create a theater for the people. Her individual style of direction and production involved close cooperation between director, writer and actors and detailed research into the period of the play combined with lengthy rehearsals.

Anti-war, the production deals with the postures and prejudices and almost criminal stupidities which led to and continued the First World War.

The irony is reinforced by setting the action within the format of a seaside pierrot variety show. This popular form of entertainment was a common sight on the beaches around Britain at the beginning of the twentieth century. The show was staged either on scaffolds on the beach, or in the theater to be found at the end of the pier.

An integral part of the presentation is the positioning of screens. Slides showing events of the times are shown on the backstage wall and over the proscenium arch.

By keeping the action within the proscenium arch, more seating can be fitted and space is created for a band if required

Proscenium arch set

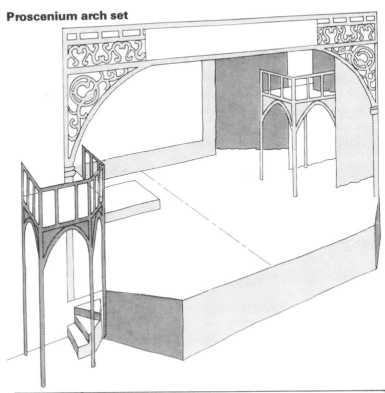

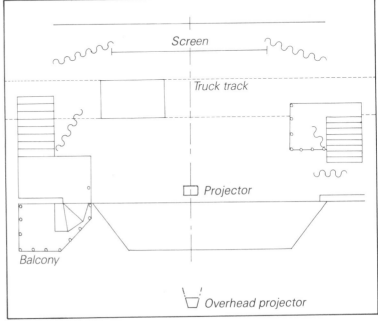

The colors should be unsophisticated — mirror the sepia tones of the slides and use black curtains to provide a stark background for the white painted ironwork which so typified the architecture of the Victorian period. Colored fairy lights underline the seaside atmosphere as do the bright pierrot costumes of the performers.

The actors change costume frequently and a well. organized wardrobe area must be situated out of sight near the stage.

The proscenium arch stage is well suited to this production. Levels, and access to them, accentuate the dramatic viewing lines. Blackouts are effective and zonal lighting is easily established. Use soft masking wherever possible. Project one of the balconies beyond the arch.

All the units illustrated will serve in both the proscenium arch or the extended apron situation. In the round presentations however can create problems with sight-lines and screen positioning.

Remove the main front curtains so that the audience is confronted with the pierrot set as soon as they take their seats. Dress the auditorium with posters of the period and dress the front of house management in appropriate costume. Make an authentic program, using the same dated lettering style for all headings and notices.

The extended apron set provides plenty of room for the cast, though valuable seating space is taken up, especially if an orchestra pit is constructed

Extended apron set

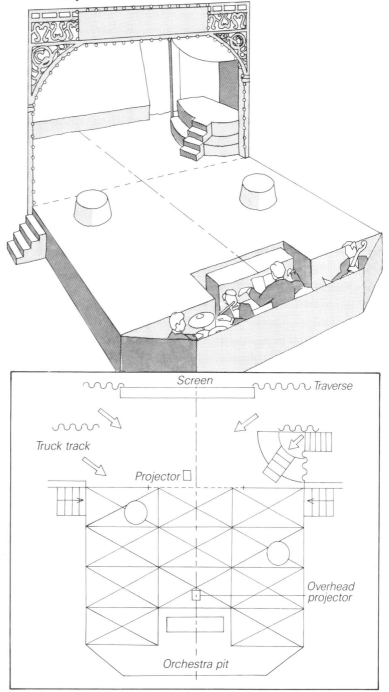

Oh what a lovely war

Covering the proscenium arch

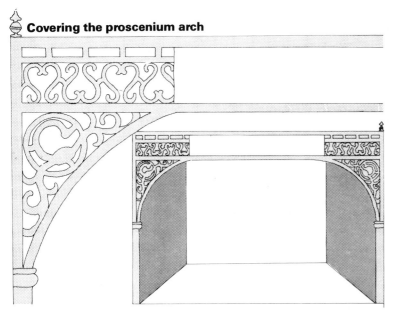

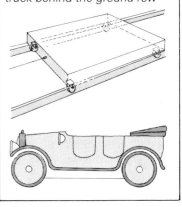

Decorate the side pillars and head of the proscenium arch with cut profiles shaped like wrought ironwork. Simple shapes may be fretted out to add lightness to the profile. Allow an appropriate space for the news panel screen situated at the center of the arch.

An angled screen

If used with front projection the back screen needs to be lifted some 3 to 4 feet (90-120cm) off the stage level and sloped, to avoid distortion of the projected images. The screen need be only of the lightest material and stretched over a light wood frame. A remotely controlled projector can be suspended behind a border or the proscenium arch. (Tape a line down stage of the screen so that the actors behind do not obstruct the projection.)

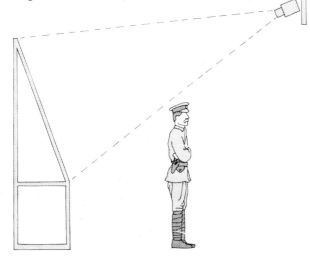

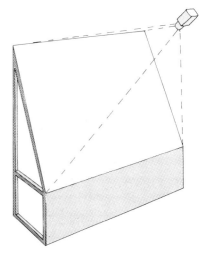

Circus tubs

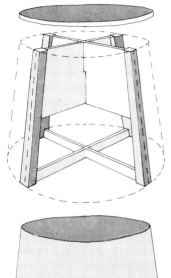

Simple brightly painted tubs can be used as seats or small platforms. If castered these can easily be re-positioned. Cover with curved hardboard panels

Bandstand roof

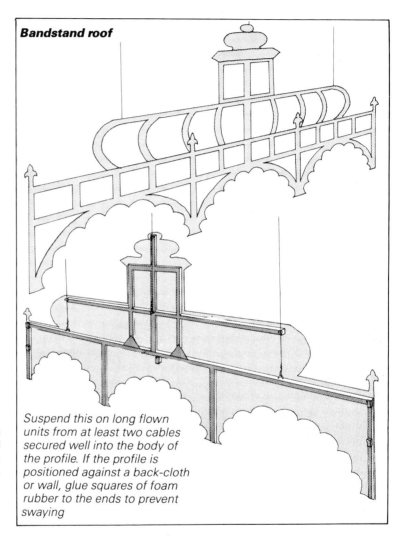

Suspend this on long flown units from at least two cables secured well into the body of the profile. If the profile is positioned against a back-cloth or wall, glue squares of foam rubber to the ends to prevent swaying

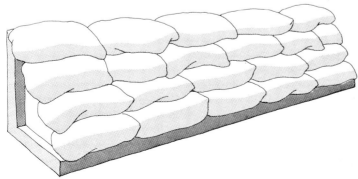

Sandbag ground row

Construct a ground row so that the downstage face is sloping at a 45° angle. Make simple shapes from papier mâché, and glue these to the hardboard surface. Add sawdust to stage paint to give the 'bags' a grainy, rough texture.

Glossary

Acting area The area of the stage in which the actors perform

Apron Part of the stage projecting into the auditorium in front of the house curtains

Auditorium The audience area beyond the stage

Back-cloth or Back-drop A scene canvas across the width of the stage fixed at top and bottom

Backstage The non-acting area behind the proscenium arch

Bar or Barrel Iron piping above stage for lighting and scenery

Batten Scenic wood lengths for tautening cloth at top or bottom or timber used to join flats

Block or head block Pulley bearing lines for flying scenery

Book flat A hinged flat

Border A horizontally placed flat or cloth hung from bar or ceiling grid to mask lights and flown scenery from the audience

Box set A room setting with only three walls

Brace Extending rod angled to support flats. Used with stage weight or stage screw

Brace cleat Attachment on the back of a flat to which the stage brace is hooked

Brail The rope and adjusting part of hanging scenery

Center line A line running through the exact center of the proscenium arch

Cleat Fitting on flats to which throw lines are secured

Cloth Area of scenic canvas hanging vertically

Cut cloth Parts cut away for foliage effect etc.

Cut-out flat A shaped flat in plywood or hardboard

Cyclorama or sky-cloth Either a smooth plastered wall or a stretched, curved or straight back-cloth. Painted white and lit

Deck Storage area

Dolly A small truck

Down stage The area of stage nearest the audience

Draw line Operating line of a traverse curtain

Edge up To raise a piece of scenery up-right on its edge

Elevation Scale drawing of a side view of stage or stage unit

False proscenium A temporary arrangement of flats or cloths behind the main arch to reduce the overall dimensions of the arch, and makes the stage area smaller

Flat Standard unit of scenery with a wooden frame and canvas, plywood or hardboard covering

Flies Space above the stage where scenery is hung out of sight

Floodlights/floods Fixed wide angle general spread lighting units, used for illuminating large areas of the stage or cyclorama

Floor cloth Canvas floor covering

Floor plan Scale drawing of exact positioning of openings

Flown Housed in flies

Fore and aft Measuring the length rather than width of stage

Fore stage The area immediately in front of the house curtain

French brace Supporting bracket hinged and folded for storage

Front cloth Hung well down stage so scenery can be changed behind it

Gauze or scrim Loosely-woven fabric which becomes transparent or opaque when appropriately lit

Gelatine/gel A color filter for lighting

Grid Wood or metal flats bearing pulley blocks

Ground plan A scaled drawing of a setting seen from above

Ground row Shaped pieces of standing scenery 2-3 feet (60-90cm) high

Grouping The arrangement of actors in and around the set

Hemp Rope used for flying

House Everything beyond the stage

House curtain The main curtain in a proscenium theater

House lights Auditorium lighting

Interior A scene set indoors

Kill Removing props from a set

Ladder A non-climbable frame used for positioning lights

Left stage or stage left The area on the left of an actor facing the audience

Leg Long narrow strip of fabric. Black for masking

Levels Rostra, ramps and steps above the main stage

Lines Hemp ropes for raising and lowering scenery

Mahl-stick A rod padded at one end to steady the painting hand

Marking Laying out colored tape to mark the position of scenery

Masking Hiding lights or the backstage area from view

Off stage Space outside the performance area

On stage Inside the performance area

O.P. Opposite prompt or 'stage right'

Plate A triangular plywood reinforcing corner for flats

Plot General list required by all departments noting exact requirements and cues

Profile flat Alternative to the cut-out flat

Props Properties — anything used on stage (not scenery, wardrobe, light or sound)

Proscenium The wall dividing the audience from the stage area

P.S. Prompt side — stage left

Rail Bottom or top batten in a flat construction

Rake Sloped auditorium or stage to facilitate viewing

Return A flat leading off at right angles to another

Reveal A small 'return' surrounding an arch, window or doorway to suggest thickness

Risers The vertical part of a step

Roller Mechanism for hanging canvas cloth

Rostrum A platform

Run Horizontal width of step

Scrim See gauze

Seque An immediate follow-on in a show

Set To prepare the stage for all the scenery and furniture used

Setting line A line normally parallel to the front of the stage just up stage from the curtain line

Sight-lines Lines on a plan or elevation indicating the limits of what an audience can see

Sill An iron bar screwed to the bottom of a door flat to secure it to the stage floor

Sky-cloth See Cyclorama

Stage screw A screw for fixing braces to strong stage floors

Stage weight Used to secure the base of a stage brace

Stile Vertical batten in the framework of a flat

Strike the set Dismantling scenery

Tab Curtain — front tabs are the main house curtains

Teaser A short masking drop

Three fold Three flats hinged together

Throw line A rope which interconnects stage flats

Toggle or bar Cross piece in a flat frame

Tormentor Narrow curtain used to mask wings sometimes at right angles to the proscenium arch

Trap A door in the stage floor of large theaters, used for special effects and entrances

Traverse Tabs set on a track across the stage

Trim Scenery or masking hanging parallel to the stage

Truck or wagon A mobile platform for scenery

Up stage The area of the stage furthest from the audience

Wagon See Truck

Wing curtains The soft masking of the wing space

Wings The area to either side of the acting area

Index